BOEING 707

A Legends of Flight Illustrated History

WOLFGANG BORGMANN

SCHIFFER MILITARY

4880 Lower Valley Road   Atglen, PA 19310

Originally published as *Die Flugzeugstars: Boeing 707* by Motorbuch Verlag © 2019 Motorbuch Verlag
Translated from the German by David Johnston

Library of Congress Control Number: 2021942741

Designed by Justin Watkinson
Cover design by Molly Shields
Type set in DIN/Minion Pro

ISBN: 978-0-7643-6345-0
Printed in India

Published by Schiffer Publishing, Ltd.
4880 Lower Valley Road
Atglen, PA 19310
Phone: (610) 593-1777; Fax: (610) 593-2002
Email: Info@schifferbooks.com
Web: www.schifferbooks.com

For our complete selection of fine books on this and related subjects, please visit our website at www.schifferbooks.com. You may also write for a free catalog.

Schiffer Publishing's titles are available at special discounts for bulk purchases for sales promotions or premiums. Special editions, including personalized covers, corporate imprints, and excerpts, can be created in large quantities for special needs. For more information, contact the publisher.

We are always looking for people to write books on new and related subjects. If you have an idea for a book, please contact us at proposals@schifferbooks.com.

CONTENTS

This close-up of an American Airlines Boeing 707-320C was taken at Los Angeles International Airport. *Bob Proctor*

INTRODUCTION

This book tells the story of the Boeing 707 and 720 airliners and the 367-80 prototype, the Dash 80. The parallel military models, the Boeing 717 (KC-135) and Boeing E-3 Sentry, are therefore considered only in the historical context of the development and operational history of the civilian 707.

Despite this, a separate chapter is dedicated to the four Boeing jets operated by the Luftwaffe, which between 1968 and 1999 not only carried government officials and military VIPs but also delivered humanitarian disaster relief aid around the globe. Although these were military aircraft, they were built with a civilian Boeing construction number as the 707-307C.

In the course of their service lives, the 725 examples of the civil Boeing 707 produced between 1957 and 1978, and the 154 Boeing 720s that were built, flew with countless well- and lesser-known airlines on all five continents. To describe them all would exceed the scope of this book. Therefore, the description of this intercontinental jet's history will focus on its service with Lufthansa, its former charter subsidiary Condor, the Luftwaffe's executive transport flight, and various smaller airlines in German-speaking countries, which often flew 707s and 720s for just a short time.

Two Boeing 707s, owned by Lufthansa and Pan American, on the ramp at the Kai Tak airport in Hong Kong in 1961. The airport was replaced by the new Chek Lap Kok airport in 1998. The airport of the former British crown colony was then as now an air travel crossroads, and for a long time a meeting place for the worldwide 707 fleets. *Lufthansa*

FOREWORD
THE LUCKY NUMBER 7

WE'RE GOING TO MAKE THE BEST IMPRESSION ON THE TRAVELING PUBLIC, AND WE'RE GOING TO MAKE A PILE OF EXTRA DOUGH JUST FROM BEING FIRST.

—C. R. Smith, president of American Airlines, speaking in 1956 about the imminent introduction of the Boeing 707

In 1969 Austrian Airlines leased a Boeing 707 from the Belgian airline Sabena for scheduled flights between Vienna and New York. The service was not an economic success, however, and the aircraft was returned to Sabena after just two years. *Austrian Airlines*

It was no more and no less than the future of the company that was at stake when the Boeing board of directors around president Bill Allen authorized the then-unimaginable sum of sixteen million dollars for development of the 707 prototype, the 367-80 or Dash 80. After all, it represented the entire profit Boeing had made on its predominantly military aircraft models since 1945. But Allen and his team were tired of being dependent on US military contracts and sought to gain a sustainable foothold in the highly competitive airline market. Boeing had already made a name for itself in the civilian market in the prewar days with the 247 and 307 Stratoliner models and the 314 flying boats, and in 1946 the company continued this tradition with the Boeing 377 Stratocruiser.

Douglas and Lockheed dominated the civil aircraft business in the postwar period, but the cards were reshuffled when, in 1945, Boeing aerodynamicists discovered research documents concerning the design of high-speed jet aircraft with swept wings in the ruins of the Third Reich. On the basis of this highly explosive booty, Boeing developed

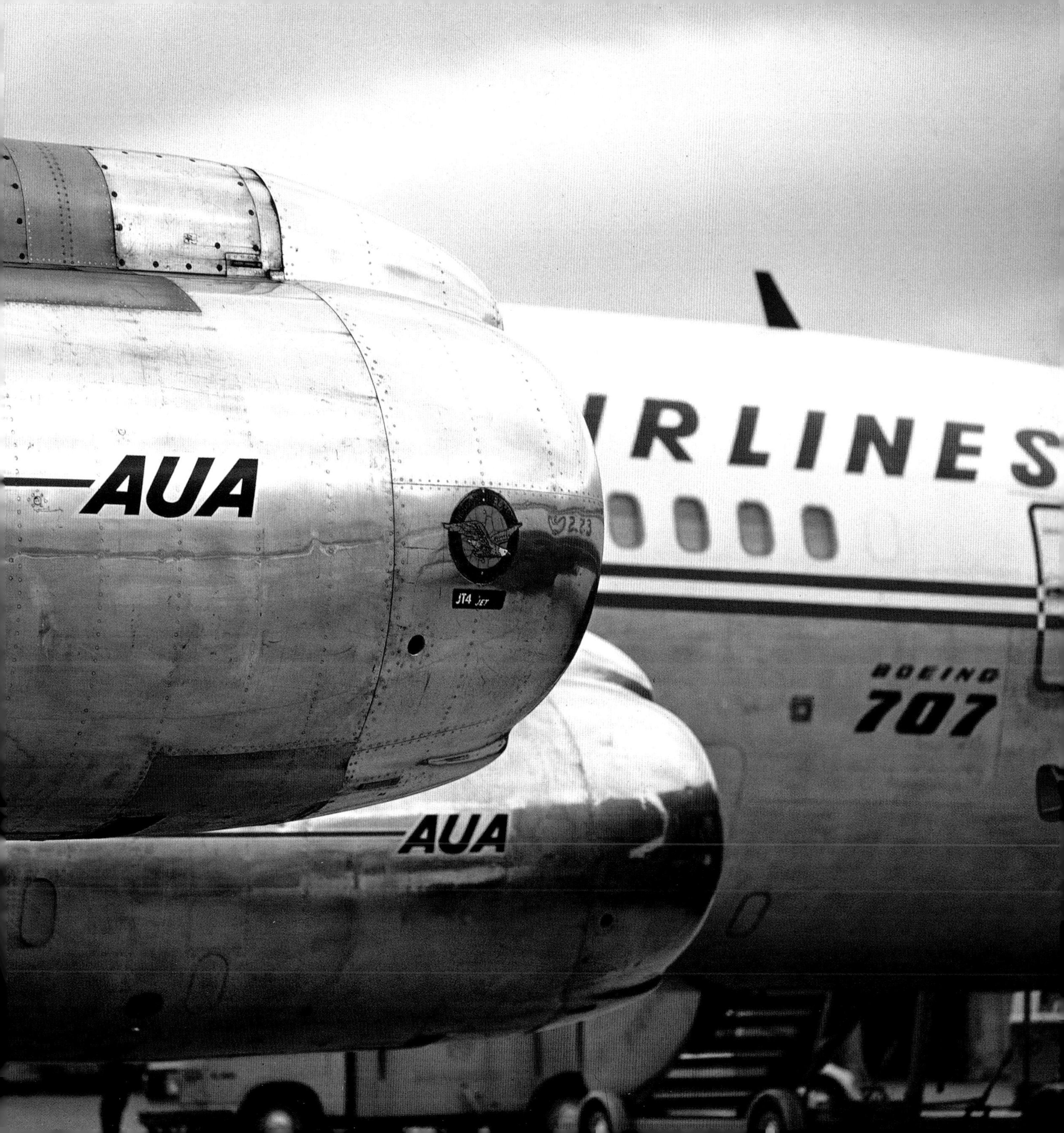
AUA
JT4 JET
IRLINES
BOEING
707
AUA

increasingly sophisticated aerodynamic designs in its own high-speed wind tunnel, which led to the B-47 and B-52 bombers. Then, on the basis of the experience gained in the process, the designers ventured to create a new jet-powered airliner in 1949. The Boeing engineers investigated the most-diverse configurations of high- and low-wing aircraft. What took shape on the drawing boards of the design department was so revolutionary that Boeing initially wanted the public to think that it was no more than an improved version of the Model 367 Stratofreighter propeller-driven aircraft. The result was the at-first-glance-confusing type nomenclature 367-80 with which Boeing designated the Dash 80 prototype. The astonishment and enthusiasm were all the greater when the future of air transport rolled out of the final assembly hangar at Renton in 1954. Even if the Dash 80 differed from the later 707 production aircraft in some respects, with its four jet engines suspended beneath the wings, it established the image of a modern jet airliner that still prevails in the public mind today. This may also be due to the fact that various design elements, such as the shape of the cockpit and cabin windows themselves, are still in use today even in the latest versions of Boeing's bestselling 737.

After the initial order from Pan Am, Boeing needed some patience until sales of the Boeing 707, developed from the Dash 80, began to pick up noticeably. For a while it even looked as if Douglas and its DC-8 would steal the show from the new Boeing.

But within a few years, the long-established Seattle-based company's design beat out Douglas and all other Western manufacturers of four-engine long-haul jets. This was due in no small part to the design of its cabin, whose more than one hundred windows allowed sunlight to flood into the cabin at cruising altitude on daytime flights.

After completing its flight test program, the Boeing 367-80, which had been signed over to the Smithsonian Air & Space Museum in 1972, was initially mothballed at Davis-Monthan Air Force Base, near Tucson, Arizona. Defying the rattlesnakes lurking in the tall grass, the photographer took this photo of the historic aircraft in 1978. *Jon Proctor*

On October 26, 1958, launch customer Pan American World Airways entered the jet age on the North Atlantic with its first 707-120s. Although British Overseas Airways Corporation (BOAC) beat it by a few days with its two maiden flights between London and New York on October 4, 1958, the American jet quickly demonstrated its operational and economic superiority over the de Havilland Comet, operated by BOAC.

Boeing took the wishes of its airline customers seriously and built customized jets with optimized jet engines for Quantas of Australia and the American carriers Braniff and United Air Lines. The result was a whole family of aircraft for medium-haul routes, transcontinental connections across the United States, intercontinental routes across oceans, and ultra-long-haul routes.

What they all have in common is the designation "707," whose genesis has more-pragmatic reasons than is often assumed. After the end of the Second World War, Boeing management decided not only to diversify its range of products but also to assign them new model numbers. The numbers 300 and 400 were henceforth reserved for military aircraft, 500 was the designation for jet engines, 600 was assigned to missiles and rockets, and 700 was the numerical series for passenger jets. An ascending-model series starting with 700, followed by 701, 702, and so on, seemed not succinct enough for the Boeing marketing experts, so they came up with the 7-7 series. This began not with 707 but with the 717, the internal company code for the tanker that the US military designated the KC-135. The reason for giving a military jet a civilian model number lay in Boeing's original plans for the 717 not only as the military KC-135, but also as a civilian airliner without any design changes. Four decades later, Boeing again reassigned the designation 717 to an aircraft type, after the MD-95, a derivative of the Douglas DC-9, was integrated into its own portfolio following the merger with McDonnell Douglas.

The third exception to the rule was the model 720. Originally offered by Boeing as the 707-020, launch customer United Air Lines insisted that it be renamed, since it had already acquired the competing DC-8. The company did not want the public to interpret the purchase of the Douglas jet as a mistake, so Boeing changed the model number from 707-020 to 720 for what was supposed to be a completely new aircraft type. This allowed United managers to save face and tout the DC-8 and the 720 as the two best jets of their time.

Not until the summer of 2013 did the Iranian airline Saha Air retire its two Boeing 707s, the last in airline service anywhere in the world, fifty-five years after Pan American had taken off into the jet age with this aircraft type.

The number 7 was to prove a fortunate choice for Boeing, in that combined sales of the model 717, 707, 720, 727, 737-747, 757, 767, 777, 717, and 787 series have made the company number one in the world in the production of civil aircraft.

Now fasten your seat belts for a nonstop flight through the fascinating history of the Boeing intercontinental jet.

Wolfgang Borgmann
Oerlinghausen, autumn 2021

Pilot and copilot carrying their preflight checks in the cockpit of a Lufthansa Boeing 707 in 1968. The flight engineer, the third member of the cockpit crew, is outside carrying out the preflight "walk-around." *Lufthansa*

CHAPTER 1
THE SWEPT WING
GERMAN KNOW-HOW, NOT JUST FOR BOEING JETS

The Italian physicist Allessandro Giuseppe Antonio Anastasio Volta (1745–1827) is regarded as the inventor of the electric battery and is one of the founders of the theory of electricity. The unit of measurement for electrical voltage was named after him. Volta was posthumously awarded one of the greatest possible honors in science. In 1927, the Royal Italian Academy of Sciences established the Allessandro Volta Foundation, which to this day promotes the exchange of ideas among researchers from all over the world.

The fifth forum of experts organized by the academy and attended by the leading minds in aeronautics research took place in Rome from September 30 to October 6, 1935, and dealt with the current state of the theoretical foundations of high-speed flight. Among the participants at this Fifth VOLTA Congress on High-Speed Flight was the German aerodynamicist Adolf Busemann. At the suggestion

Historical transcript of the lecture given by Maurice Roy at the 5th VOLTA Congress on High-Speed Flight. Like Adolf Busemann of Germany, the French scientist conducted research into high-speed flight and presented these results in a detailed paper in Rome in 1935. *Author's archive*

of Professor Ludwig Prandtl, head of the Aerodynamic Research Institute (AVA) at Göttingen, at the congress he presented for the first time the highly regarded thesis on the advantages of swept wings in high-speed flight. Busemann's idea was far ahead of its time and was ultimately further developed in German research laboratories, with the aim of specific applications. One of the centers for swept-wing research in Germany was the AVA, where, in 1937, experiments conducted by graduate physicist Hubert Ludwieg succeeded in proving Busemann's swept-wing theory for the first time. Busemann himself was appointed head of the newly created Institute for Gas Dynamics at the Brunswick-Völkenrode Aviation Research Institute (LFA), where he continued to devote himself to swept-wing research. Within a short time, high-speed wind tunnels were created by the

LFA in Brunswick, the AVA in Göttingen, and the Berlin-based German Aviation Research Institute (DVL), where increasingly detailed studies were conducted into the optimal design of swept wings. One of the results was the "Krueger flap," named after its inventor Werner Krüger, which not only was installed as a lift-generating leading-edge flap on the Boeing 707 and 720 but is still found today on many modern commercial aircraft. In 1944, the AVA patented Krüger's invention as a "high-lift device for airfoils with an arbitrarily small leading-edge radius." Thanks to the jet propulsion systems being developed in Germany at the same time, theoretical calculations and model tests did not stop there. One of the first types to be built with a swept wing was the four-engine Junkers Ju 287 bomber, which first flew on August 16, 1944. It had forward-swept wings, which its designer Hans-Heinrich Wocke would again use from 1964 onward on the Hansa Jet, produced by the Hamburger Flugzeugbau GmbH. The Ju 287 was the first jet to be designed according to the "transonic area rule," which Junkers engineer Otto Frenzl discovered in 1943 and the Junkers Flugzeugwerke patented in 1944. This rule describes the optimum distribution of the aircraft cross section, which in a jet should be evenly distributed like a parabola on the x/y-axis from the nose toward the tail. Since the cross section is greatest in the area of the wing with the engines and airfoils—thus destroying the optimal parabolic shape—in order to compensate for this, aircraft designed according to the area rule often

This drawing of the HFB 320 Hansa Jet designed by Hans-Heinrich Wocke in the early 1960s reveals its layout, with a "wasp waist" to reduce the aircraft cross section in accordance with the transonic area rule discovered by Frenzl. *Author's archive*

A NASA Lockheed SR-71 refueling in flight from a Boeing KC-135 tanker. It was standard procedure for the SR-71 to take off with a minimum fuel load and refuel in the air, before carrying out its mission at up to three times the speed of sound. To be able to reach these extremely high speeds, the SR-71 was designed with an extremely narrow fuselage in the area of maximum wingspan, according to the transonic area rule. *NASA / Lori Losey*

have a fuselage cross section that is tapered in places, resulting in a so-called wasp waist.

Although the Junkers patent continued to exist after 1945, this rule was initially forgotten in the postwar turmoil. It was only after the American physicist Richard T. Whitcomb of the National Advisory Committee for Aeronautics (NACA) discovered it for the second time about ten years after Frenzl and named it the "area rule" that this principle finally found its way into aircraft design. The concrete effects of the application of the area rule are illustrated by the example of the American Convair F-102 jet fighter, developed in the early 1950s. As originally designed, the jet was unable to break the sound barrier, but after it was modified with Frenzl and Whitcomb's "wasp waist" and was incorporated into the design, it succeeded in doing so without difficulty.

The extent to which the development of swept wings had progressed in Germany by the end of the war was revealed to the victorious Allies only after the discovery of the laboratories at Völkenrode in 1945. Under the direction of the leading American aerodynamicist Theodore von Kármán, American troops secured the booty found there. By 1946, there had accumulated a mountain of paper weighing about 1,200 tons, containing all the information about the German aerospace industry of the time. The next step was to evaluate it in the United States and make it available for use by the domestic aviation industry. In addition to documents, the American military also brought captured aircraft and German scientists to America. Rocket experts in particular were forcibly relocated overseas as part of Operation Overcast and Operation Paperclip in order to give up their expertise.

Wernher von Braun, who, in the years that followed, built the US space program and made America the first nation to reach the moon, became a legend. Among the experts, however, there were also scientists from Völkenrode who became involved in American aviation research. One of them was Dr. Adolf Busemann, who worked for the Royal Aircraft Establishment in Farnborough in 1946, and then from 1947 onward at the Langley Research Center in the United States. He also remained in the country after his enforced stay in the United States, and in 1963 he was appointed professor at the University of Colorado in Boulder, where he remained until his death on November 3, 1983.

ON THE WAY TO THE 707

Boeing chief aerodynamicist George S. Schairer was part of the team led by Theodore von Kármán that inspected the facilities at Völkenrode in 1945. There he and Kármán met Dr. Adolf Busemann for the very first time and were briefed on the state of German swept-wing research firsthand. Schairer immediately recognized the explosive nature of Busemann's information and the booty the Americans had found, and in May 1945 he reported to his colleagues in Seattle on the discoveries made at Völkenrode. After his return to the United States, Schairer called a halt to developmental work on the B-47 straight-wing bomber, which had been in planning since 1943, in favor of a jet with swept wings based on the German research documents. The concept was further refined in the Boeing high-speed wind tunnel, and on December 17, 1947, the Boeing model 450-3-3 (XB-47), the first American swept-wing jet bomber, flew for the first time. The fundamental research carried out by Boeing for the XB-47, on the basis of captured German documents, not only gave the Seattle-based aircraft manufacturer an immense competitive edge but also paved the way to the modern jet aircraft—and thus to the Boeing 707.

Ten years after its initial discovery by Germany's Otto Frenzl, the American physicist Richard T. Whitcomb of the National Advisory Committee for Aeronautics (NACA) rediscovered his transonic area rule. He also developed the idea of "winglets" to reduce wingtip vortices and achieve reduced fuel consumption. The first flight trials were carried out by a Boeing KC-135 stationed at the NASA research airfield at Dryden in 1979 and 1980. The trials revealed a 7 percent reduction in fuel consumption compared to the standard KC-135. This was the starting signal for today's common application on commercial aircraft and business jets. *NASA*

A Boeing B-47A on the ramp of the NACA High Speed Research Station at Edwards Air Force Base in California in 1953. Powered by six General Electric J-47-GE-23 turbojets, the B-47 was the United States' first swept-wing jet bomber. Its design was based on German research results that Boeing engineers found at Völkenrode, near Brunswick, after the surrender of the Third Reich. *NASA*

In 2002, NASA procured a second Boeing B-52 for flight trials. It is seen here on display at the Boeing factory in Wichita during celebrations marking the B-52's fiftieth anniversary. First flown on April 15, 1952, with its swept wings the B-52 was another development step on the path to the Boeing 707. *NASA / Tony Landis*

The wing of the Boeing 707 had 35 degrees of sweep, on the basis of the results of German research obtained between 1935 and 1945. *Boeing*

CHAPTER 2
THE DE HAVILLAND COMET
PIONEER OF JET AIR TRAVEL

The first flight by the de Havilland D.H. 106 Comet on July 27, 1949, marked the beginning of the jet age in commercial air travel. During this historic flight, chief pilot John Cunningham flew the prototype, wearing the class B markings G-5-1 (later G-ALVG), for all of thirty-one minutes before returning it safely to the factory airfield at Hatfield. The second prototype, with the class B markings G-5-2 (later G-ALZK), took to the air exactly one year later. With the two prototypes, the company carried out an extensive flight test program, which culminated in a certificate of airworthiness from the British aviation authority.

With the Comet, an aircraft that flew almost twice as fast and twice as high as any other airliner of its day, de Havilland designers broke new ground in the fields of design, navigation, meteorology, and ground handling. The task of ensuring an adequate supply of the jet fuel needed by the aircraft's four Ghost gas turbines at the D.H. 106's destination and alternate airports was also an immense logistical challenge.

The de Havilland designers were aware that transporting forty passengers at altitudes of up to 39,370 ft. would place extremely high demands on the structure of the pressurized cabin. To leave nothing to chance, de Havilland built a large water tank in which the individual fuselage sections of the Comet were pressure-tested to the bursting point. In the process, the manufacturer voluntarily worked with a cabin pressure that was two and a half times higher than the value required by the British licensing authority. The cabin windows were even tested at ten times the safety factor!

As a further precautionary measure, de Havilland set up a cryogenic pressure chamber in which a Comet fuselage, including components, was subjected to simulated flight altitudes of up to 68,897 ft. and a temperature of minus 70 degrees Celsius (–94° Fahrenheit). It soon became apparent that various materials commonly used in aviation up to that time were unsuitable for the D.H. 106's planned flight altitudes and had to be replaced with new ones.

At 3:12 p.m. on the afternoon of May 2, 1952, BOAC formally opened the "jet age." On that day the Comet 1, with the registration G-ALYP, took off from London airport on the first scheduled jet flight in aviation history. Because of the relatively short range of the Comet 1, the aircraft had to make five refueling stops on its way from Great Britain to South Africa. Consequently, it took twenty-three hours and thirty-seven minutes for aircraft Yoke Peter to finally reach its destination of Johannesburg, South Africa. "Three minutes before the scheduled arrival time," as the de Havilland staff newspaper from June 1952 proudly noted. The smooth flight made possible by the new jet engines so delighted the first Comet passengers that balancing a coin on its edge or building houses of cards—completely impossible in flight in old propeller-driven airliners with their shaking piston engines—became a common onboard activity!

At first it seemed as if nothing could stop the Comet's success. Representatives of the world's leading airlines flocked to de Havilland. A second final-assembly line was planned at Chester, in addition to the one at Hatfield, to produce aircraft to fill the numerous orders. In addition to the launch customer BOAC, the airlines Air India, Air France, British Commonwealth Pacific Airlines, Canadian Pacific, Japan Air Lines, Linea Aeropostal Venezolana, Pan American World Airways, Panair do Brasil, and UTA all placed orders for Comet versions 1A, 2, and 3.

Two takeoff accidents involving BOAC and Canadian Pacific aircraft were the ominous harbingers of what was to happen shortly afterward. While these accidents could still be explained by a lack of jet experience on the part of their pilots, fate struck again on May 2, 1953. Just six minutes after taking off from Calcutta, BOAC Comet 1 G-ALYV broke up in flight, which the investigating authorities attributed to severe turbulence in a thunderstorm. None of the six crew members and thirty-seven passengers survived the disaster. As a consequence of this accident, BOAC equipped all its Comet aircraft with weather radar for the detection of storms.

The accident in Karachi had almost been forgotten when news of the crash of the BOAC Comet 1 G-ALYP flashed around the world. Radio communication with the aircraft, which had just taken off from Rome, was lost at an altitude of about 26,575 ft. Italian fishermen saw burning debris falling out of the sky into the sea, but even a prompt rescue operation failed to recover a single survivor. Those responsible were initially puzzled over the cause of the

A Comet 1 of British Overseas Airways Corporation (BOAC) launched the jet age on May 2, 1952. *Dave Robinson collection*

Nueva York a Cuatro Horas y Media de Caracas

LINEA AEROPOSTAL VENEZOLANA HAS CHOSEN THE COMET
(Series 2 with Rolls-Royce Avon engines)

Linea Aeropostal Venezolana was one of many airlines that planned to take off into the jet age with the Comet 2. These plans were frustrated, however, after the D.H. 106's type certification was withdrawn on April 12, 1954. *Dave Robinson collection*

accident. The "black boxes" standard in modern aircraft, which record cockpit conversations and flight data, were not yet standard equipment in commercial aircraft. To be on the safe side, BOAC temporarily grounded its Comet fleet and awaited the outcome of the accident investigation. In the end, the investigators concluded that the most probable cause of the accident was the failure of the fan blade assembly in one of the Ghost engines. After more than fifty technical modifications, BOAC resumed flight operations with its Comet 1s on March 23, 1954.

With no clear cause found for the accident, aviation experts were still speculating about the crash of G-ALYP when the events of January were tragically repeated on April 8, 1954. Once again it was a Comet 1, and once again Rome was the departure airport. South African Airways had chartered G-ALYY from BOAC at the time, and flight SA201 was climbing south after taking off from the Italian capital. Once again, as in the crash of G-ALYP, the seven crew members and fourteen passengers had no chance of survival. The crew again did not have time to make a distress call, and the aircraft seemed to mysteriously disintegrate within seconds, as in the crash four months earlier.

This time the authorities reacted more consistently, and the D.H. 106 series' certificate of airworthiness was revoked on April 12, 1954. In an unprecedented salvage operation, with the support of the British Royal Navy, a large part of the wrecked G-ALYY structure was fished out of the Mediterranean Sea and reassembled on the grounds of the Royal Aircraft Establishment (RAE), then an aviation research facility, at Farnborough, England. Within six weeks, a 111.5 by 19.7 ft. water tank was built to accommodate the complete fuselage of the BOAC Comet 1 G-ALYU for a load test. This was the first test of a complete fuselage, since de Havilland had previously tested only individual fuselage sections. In addition, the cabin windows of the prototypes had been bonded to the structure with the special aerospace adhesive Redux, while those of the production aircraft operated by BOAC were fastened to the structure with punch rivets. At the same time, the Comet 1 G-ANAV was subjected to a rigorous flight test program to identify any deficiencies in the Comet's flight behavior.

The tests under the direction of Sir Arnold Hall, chairman of the RAE, finally produced the answer: metal fatigue had led to the bursting of the Comet fuselages—with fatal consequences for the passengers and crews. The subsequent public hearing ended with the realization that the de Havilland engineers had gone so far into new technological territory that they could not foresee the dangers. In order to prevent similar catastrophes, the British authorities made the investigation report with all the technical details public. This knowledge, gained at the cost of tragedy, flowed directly into the designs of the Boeing 707 and Douglas DC-8. One consequence of the events of 1953 and 1954 was the design of all subsequent commercial aircraft according to the so-called "fail safe" principle. This philosophy of fail-safe design dictated that the failure of a particular component must not lead to failure of the entire system. Rather, another component must be able to take over its function at least until the next routine check. To prevent catastrophes, crack stoppers ensure that damage does not spread uncontrollably through the structure and lead to failure. As a result of the Comet series of accidents, flying has also become a great deal safer.

The de Havilland company placed great hopes in the Comet 3, the first long-range version of the airliner, which was also supposed to fly to India. Even though the Comet 3 never flew commercially due to its weakly designed structure, its design formed the aerodynamic basis for the later Comet 4, which was operated successfully. *Dave Robinson collection*

BOAC operated its Comet 4b airliners from London-Heathrow to North America and to Australia. Hong Kong was one of the many refueling stopovers on the way to the fifth continent. *Dave Robinson collection*

CHAPTER 3
FROM THE DASH 80 TO THE 707 INTERCONTINENTAL JET

I WAS SELLING THE AIRPLANE.

—Boeing test pilot Tex Johnston's reply to Boeing president Bill Allen, when he asked what Johnston had been thinking when he carried out a barrel roll in the Dash 80 before the assembled press

When the Boeing 367-80 Dash 80 was presented to the world public on May 14, 1954, no one present could have imagined that its design would remain the standard for aircraft construction to this day. Not only visually, but also technologically, numerous Boeing jets of the modern era have their roots in this pioneering test aircraft of the early 1950s. The design of the Dash 80, with its wings swept 35 degrees and the engines mounted on pylons under the wings, also shaped the public's idea of what a modern passenger jet should look like. As the ancestor of the Boeing 707 as well as the 720/727/737 family of aircraft, the Dash 80 still seems up to date even today and would hardly strike most observers as a sixty-five-year-old jet on a current-day airport apron.

Boeing used its 367-80 on the one hand as a research aircraft, to collect important data for the design of passenger aircraft, but also as a demonstration aircraft for potential customers. And so, not only managers but also pilots and engineers from the world's leading airlines made their way to Seattle.

Among them was the charismatic Pan American founder and president Juan T. Trippe, who was looking for a suitable aircraft type with which to take his airline into the jet age. Just one month before the rollout of the Dash 80, his dream of flying away from the competition with three de Havilland D.H. 106 Comet 3 long-range jets had come to nothing after the Comet lost its type certification in April 1954 as a result of fatal design flaws. The first preliminary designs for the Boeing jetliner from 1949 still bore a strong resemblance to Boeing's own B-47. After detailed studies, Boeing engineers quickly rejected the concept of a shoulder-wing aircraft for the planned new passenger jet. The arrangement of its systems and the landing gear seemed too complex. On April 22, 1952, the Boeing board of directors officially authorized construction of the 367-80. The low-wing design chosen for the Dash 80 allowed, for example, the flight control cables and electrical supply lines to be installed between the cabin floor and the cargo compartment below to save space, which would not have been possible with a high-wing layout. After about thirty studies, whose practicality was tested in Boeing's own high-speed wind tunnel, the Dash 80 design crystallized, and even the then-seventy-two-year-old company founder William Boeing was present for the official rollout. His wife, Bertha, christened the

A Lufthansa Boeing 707-430 lifts off from the Hamburg-Fuhlsbüttel
airport's runway 23, having used almost its entire length to get airborne.
Hamburg Airport

Ceremonial rollout of the Boeing 367-80 at the Boeing company airfield at Renton, near Seattle, on May 14, 1954. Even company founder William Boeing and his wife, Bertha, attended the festivities. *Boeing*

aircraft with a bottle of "real champagne," as the Boeing chronicle notes.

In order to initially conceal that it was developing a jet airliner, Boeing used the type designation 367-80 to give the appearance that the Dash 80 was merely an improved version of the Boeing 367 Stratofreighter. But the jet transport aircraft unveiled at Renton had nothing in common with a conventional propeller-driven aircraft. The public presentation was followed on July 15, 1954, by the widely acclaimed maiden flight of the Dash 80. The experts were enthusiastic, but the airlines were reluctant to place firm orders for the 707 jetliner, which had been developed from the 367-80. Archrival Douglas in Long Beach, California, was not innocent in this. At the time, the traditional family-owned company was considered a leader in civil aircraft design. Its success story had begun in 1933 with the DC-1 and, following the DC-2, DC-3, and DC-5, continued in the postwar period with the great DC-4, DC-6, and DC-7. Boeing, on the other hand, was very active in the military sector and, with the exception of the Boeing 377 Stratocruiser, did not offer a single commercial aircraft in its product range after 1945. This lack of experience in meeting the wishes of the airlines may also have led to the fact that Boeing offered its first 707 variant with a narrow fuselage—in which the airlines showed no interest. In contrast to the Douglas DC-8 jet, which had a wider fuselage that could comfortably accommodate six seats per row, Boeing offered its 707 with a narrower fuselage and only five seats per row. The engineers had already widened the fuselage cross section compared to the Dash 80, but this was not yet enough to satisfy the airlines.

It was the US Department of Defense that came to the rescue, placing an initial order with Boeing for twenty-one Boeing 717 (KC-135) tanker aircraft in February 1955—an initial order that would later become 808 aircraft! The KC-135 had the same fuselage width as the civilian 707 at that time, and thanks to this military order, Boeing was able to plan and finance both projects. The first airline order was placed on October 13, 1955, by Pan American president Juan T. Trippe for twenty-five Douglas DC-8s in the

Developed in parallel to the Boeing 717 (*photo*), the Boeing 707 was originally supposed to be equipped with a maximum of five seats per row and have the narrower fuselage of its military counterpart. Under its US military designation KC-135, the Boeing 717 became famous and remains in service as an aerial-refueling tanker to this day. *NASA*

Pan American World Airways placed the first order for twenty Boeing 707s on October 13, 1955. At that point in time the type offered still had the narrow fuselage of the Boeing 717 (KC-135). *Boeing*

Potential customers could opt to purchase the Boeing 707 as a passenger jet, a combi version capable of carrying passengers or freight (or a combination of the two on the main deck), or as a pure freighter. Seen here is a Lufthansa Boeing 707-330C freighter. *Werner Krüger / Lufthansa*

"overwater" configuration, as well as twenty Boeing 707s. The Boeing's future seemed more than doubtful at the time, since, to the joy of the Douglas Aircraft Company, Trippe announced follow-up orders only for its DC-8. The words of the Pan Am founder made airline bosses around the globe sit up and take notice: the opinion of the president of the world's largest airline, who was also a general trend-setter in the industry, carried great weight.

Not only for Pan Am was the wider cabin of the Douglas jet the decisive criterion in favor of the DC-8. United Air Lines, which had worked closely with Douglas on the optimal cross section of the DC-8's fuselage, also favored the alternative jet from Long Beach. Only American Airlines succeeded in convincing Boeing's management to increase the fuselage diameter of its four-engine jet from the original 12 to 12.3 ft.—compared to the 12.2 ft. of the competing DC-8. American Airlines, a Douglas customer for decades, was convinced of the advantages of the Boeing 707 and ordered thirty aircraft on November 8, 1955. Compared to the DC-8, not only was the 707 available on the market a year earlier, but its cabin dimensions were now even larger than its Californian competitor by a few centimeters. The race for the most orders was on, and in the end it was clearly won by Boeing. While Douglas was able to sell 556 civil DC-8s, Boeing sold 754 Boeing 707s and 154 Boeing 720s (707-020). Including military variants, Boeing produced a total of 1,010 Boeing 707s and 808 examples of the 717 (KC-135) tanker. The pioneering spirit shown by then Boeing president Bill Allen in the 1950s had paid off for the company in cash and made Seattle one of the centers of civil aircraft manufacturing in the Western world.

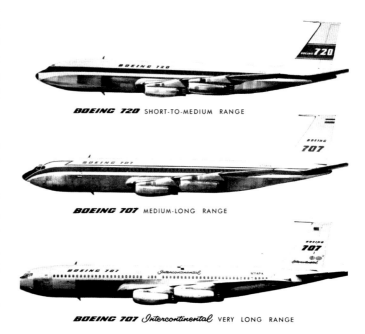

Airline profit-makers

e Boeing jetliners shown above are de-ned for profitable operations over all air-e routes, from short intercity segments to y long overocean stages.

eir outstanding earning power has already n demonstrated by the 707. Since going o service in October 1958, this Boeing jet attracted unprecedented load factors of to 95%. Operators describe it as the most pular airliner in aviation history.

e 707 Intercontinental—the world's fast-, longest-range jetliner—is now in com-rcial operation. With a range of more than 00 miles with full passenger payload, it

will fly nonstop over the longest stages of airline routes, at cruise speeds above 600 miles an hour.

The 720 is the fastest airliner of its class, with a cruise speed of 614 miles an hour. Backed by Boeing's unequalled multi-jet experience, the 720 is an extremely versatile jetliner able to operate profitably over short intercity and medium-range routes.

Boeing jetliners, now in scheduled service on United States and international routes, are demonstrating tremendous earning power, extremely high initial utilization and unprecedented public acceptance.

These airlines have already ordered Boeing jets:

AIR FRANCE · AIR-INDIA · AMERIC
B.O.A.C. · BRANIFF · CONTINENT
CUBANA · AER LINGUS · LUFTHAN
PAN AMERICAN · QANTAS · SABE2
SOUTH AFRICAN · TWA
UNITED · VARIG · Also MATS

Family of jet airliners

Boeing advertisement for its 707 and 720 family of aircraft. *Dave Robinson collection*

CHAPTER 4
BOEING 720
THE LITTLE SISTER

ONE TEST IS WORTH A THOUSAND OPINIONS.
—Tex Johnston, legendary Boeing chief test pilot

The Boeing 720 was a smaller and lighter version of the successful 707, and 154 were built between 1959 and 1967, with the Boeing 720 having succeeded in winning back United Air Lines as the launch customer for a product from Seattle, after it had not ordered the 707 but instead opted for the DC-8 made by Boeing's main competitor, Douglas. However, both the Boeing 707 and the Douglas DC-8 were too large for many domestic routes, and so the Boeing designers developed the "little sister" of the 707-120, which was 8.8 ft. shorter, at 136 ft. in length. Especially in the B version with its four Pratt & Whitney JT3D turbofan engines, the 720 showed its sporty side in flight. As former pilots of this aircraft remember, it was almost as maneuverable as a jet fighter. With a cruising speed of nearly 621 mph and a greater range, the 720B was even superior to the Convair 990 Coronado, which was especially designed for high speeds and whose thirsty General Electric engines required more-frequent refueling stops and thus lengthened overall flight time.

The 720B's increased cruising speed compared to the 707 was made possible not only by its turbofan engines but also by newly designed wings. The thickening and enlargement of the leading edge between the fuselage and the inner engine pylons, whose internal Boeing designation was "wing glove modification," in particular, led to an increase in maximum speed to Mach 0.906. In addition, Krueger flaps—leading-edge flaps—gave both versions of the 720 excellent takeoff and landing characteristics.

United put its first 720 into service on July 5, 1960, on the Chicago–Los Angeles route. Continental and Western Air Lines also operated larger fleets in the United States. The American Airlines aircraft, which the airline always marketed and marked as "707s," can be used to trace the history of the 720, which was first offered by Boeing as the 707-020. Not until it was pressed by launch customer United Air Lines is Boeing said to have agreed to the designation 720, so that United could give the impression that it had acquired a completely new aircraft type.

Servicing a Boeing 720-025 of Eastern Air Lines at New York's Idlewild airport.
Jon Proctor

A Western Air Lines Boeing 720-047B arriving at McCarran Airport, which served the gaming paradise of Las Vegas, on July 26, 1965. This aircraft, the last of three 720Bs acquired by Western after a merger with Pacific Northern Airlines, remained with the fleet until January 1980. *Jon Proctor*

With an order for eight Boeing 720Bs, Lufthansa became the first European customer for this type. *Lufthansa*

Final touches prior to delivery after a Lufthansa Boeing 720B leaves the paint hangar at Boeing's Renton plant. *Boeing*

American Airlines made no distinction between the 707 and 720B when naming its "Astrojets." Taken in 1962, this photo depicts the 720-023B with the registration N7527A, although the fuselage bears the misleading inscription "707." *Jon Proctor*

Cleared for takeoff: a Lufthansa Boeing 720B

As the first European customer, Lufthansa operated up to eight Boeing 720Bs between 1961 and 1965, using the type to replace its last four-engine, propeller-driven airliners, Lockheed L-1049G Super Constellations and L-1649A Super Stars, on its international routes. The smaller sister of the Boeing 707 set a Lufthansa internal record in January 1962, when a 720B covered the 1,890-mile route from Hong Kong to Tokyo in two hours and thirty-nine minutes. This corresponded to an average ground speed of more than 713 mph! In 1965, the Boeing 720Bs took off on the then-new flight to Australia, which had five stopovers from Frankfurt via Athens, Karachi, Bangkok, Singapore, and Darwin to Sydney as its final destination.

The Boeing 720Bs were also to be found on Lufthansa's African route network at the airports of Cairo, Lagos, Nairobi, and Johannesburg in South Africa. The Boeing 720Bs were even flown to South America and on North American transatlantic routes, such as Frankfurt–Keflavik (Iceland)–New York–Frankfurt, and Frankfurt–London–Heathrow–Montreal–San Francisco.

Alongside these great moments, the 720Bs in Lufthansa service are also associated with two tragedies in the company's history. The first, involving the aircraft with the registration D-ABOK and the name "Düsseldorf," was lost on December 4, 1961, during a training flight between Frankfurt and Cologne/Bonn, while on July 15, 1964, the second aircraft, christened "Bremen" and bearing the registration D-ABOP, crashed during a check flight by the copilot. In both cases, only the three members of the cockpit crew and no cabin crew or passengers were on board. While the first crash is still associated with a possible technical defect in the elevator trim, the second accident seems to have been caused by carelessness on the part of the pilots, because the crew executed two so-called barrel rolls. This is when the aircraft rolls about its own longitudinal axis and flies inverted for a short time. After the first barrel roll, the 720B went out of control during the second attempt and broke up in flight due to overstressing of the structure. Boeing test pilot "Tex" Johnston had performed this maneuver on August 7, 1955, flying the Boeing Dash 80 prototype, and according to reports from former Lufthansa Boeing 720B pilots, Boeing instructors on the quiet recommended the barrel roll as an alternative method of recovering from an excessively tight, steep turn. Although the crew of the D-ABOP violated Boeing and Lufthansa regulations with this maneuver, they may have thought it was safe because of the unofficial tips from the Boeing flight instructors.

After ordering Boeing 707-330Bs for long-haul and Boeing 727-030s for short- and medium-haul flights, Lufthansa took its six remaining Boeing 720s out of service in 1966 and sold the entire fleet to Pan Am. Other European customers for this type included Air Malta, Olympic Airways of Greece, and the Danish Conair of Scandinavia, which continued to operate its last Boeing 720B from Scandinavia to holiday destinations around the Mediterranean until 1987.

Fastest jetliner in its class... the Boeing 720

The short-to-medium range Boeing 720 has a higher point-to-point speed than any other jetliner in its class.

By increasing the angle of sweep-back of the 720's inboard wing, Boeing stepped up the 720's cruise speed to 614 miles an hour, and its Mach limitation number to .90.

The 720 will carry up to 130 passengers in tourist-class accommodation, and will operate economically over ranges as short as 200 miles. The 720, moreover, combines the passenger appeal of jet-speed and comfort with a lower break-even load factor than any other intermediate-range airliner.

Sister-ship of the 707, the first jet transport certified by the U.S. Civil Aeronautics Administration, the 720 incorporates the unique benefits of Boeing's 707 production experience, as well as design advances based on a continuing prototype flight-test programme.

These airlines have ordered Boeing 707 or 720 jetliners:
AIR FRANCE
AIR INDIA · AMERICAN
B.O.A.C. · BRANIFF · CONTINENTAL
CUBANA · LUFTHANSA
PAN AMERICAN · QANTAS · SABENA
SOUTH AFRICAN · TWA
UNITED · VARIG *Also* MATS

BOEING 720

Boeing ran advertisements for its 720 in aviation magazines in the 1960s.
Dave Robinson collection

A Bavarian band in traditional costume welcomes the passengers and crew of the first Lufthansa flight to Australia at the Sydney airport. The flight was made by a 720B, here surrounded on the ramp by Quantas Boeing 707-138Bs. *Lufthansa*

The short-to-medium range Boeing 720 has a higher point-to-point speed than any other jetliner in its class. By increasing the angle of sweep-back of the inboard wing, Boeing stepped up the 720's cruise speed to 614 miles an hour, and its Mach limitation number to .90.

Sister ship of the CAA-certified 707, the 720 incorporates design advances based on a continuing prototype flight-test programme. The 720 incorporates, also, all of the advantages of the experience Boeing gained in building over 1600 large, multi-jet aircraft — more than any other company in the world.

These airlines have ordered Boeing 707 and 720 jetliners:

AIR FRANCE
AIR INDIA · AMERICAN
B.O.A.C. · BRANIFF · CONTINENTAL
CUBANA · LUFTHANSA
PAN AMERICAN · QANTAS · SABENA
SOUTH AFRICAN · TWA
UNITED · VARIG · *Also* MATS

BOEING 720

A sales argument for the 720 was its high cruising speed of Mach 0.90, which Boeing advertised in this ad. *Dave Robinson collection*

Even if, with 154 aircraft sold, the Boeing 720 was not a huge sales success, Boeing was able to sell eight more of these aircraft than of its basic 707-120. Even more important, however, was the industrial significance of the 720, whose superior performance drove the Convair CV 880 and CV 990, which were its direct competitors, out of the market and brought their manufacturers to the brink of ruin. As a consequence of this economic disaster, Convair left the illustrious circle of commercial aircraft manufacturers and ceded the American four-engine aircraft market to Boeing and Douglas.

The Boeing 720B's outstanding performance, which was more like that of a fighter aircraft than a passenger jet, made it an extremely popular type among its pilots. *ETH Zurich, Swissair*

CHAPTER 5
THE CIVILIAN 707 AND 720 VARIANTS
AN OVERVIEW OF MODELS

THE PROTOTYPE

367-80 DASH 80

Prototype, first flight 1954
Just one example was built, with the telling registration N70700.

367-80B
Designation given the Dash 80 after it was fitted with Pratt & Whitney JT3D turbofan engines.

BOEING 707

707-120
The Boeing 707-120 was derived from the 367-80 and served as a template for all subsequent model variants.

The 707-120's fuselage cross section of 12.4 ft. became the standard dimension for all other models.

The base model delivered to the first customer, Pan Am, was equipped with Pratt & Whitney JT3C engines.

The wing was built with straight leading and trailing edges.

Because operations revealed that the 707 had inadequate flight stability, its vertical tail was extended by 40 inches and a ventral fin was installed beneath the tail.

707-120B
New aircraft built with JT3D turbofans, and older aircraft retrofitted with the new engines.

All of the improvements from the 720 were incorporated into this version.

A version of the 707-120 with Pratt & Whitney JT3C engines and its fuselage shortened by 9.8 ft. was produced for the Australian airline Quantas.

With two fingers extending to the fore and aft passenger doors, this Trans World Airlines Boeing 707-131B is readied for its next flight at the Los Angeles airport on February 18, 1964. *Jon Proctor*

Two retroactively modified 707-123Bs of American Airlines taxi for takeoff at the Los Angeles airport. *Bob Proctor*

707-138B

707-138 with all the improvements introduced by the 720 and 720B.

707-220

A version of the 707-120 developed and produced solely for the American airline Braniff, with more-powerful Pratt & Whitney JT4A engines for takeoffs in high temperatures and from high-elevation airfields.

First intercontinental version with lengthened fuselage, redesigned wings, and larger ail section.

The Pratt & Whitney JT4A was offered to power the aircraft.

707-320B

707-320 with further improved wings extended by 38.2 inches and Pratt & Whitney JT3D turbofan engines.

Servicing a Qantas Boeing 707-138 at New York Idlewild—the present-day John F. Kennedy Airport. In 1961, New York was a stop on Qantas's around-the-world service. *Bob Proctor*

The 707-227 version was built exclusively for Braniff. *Bob Proctor*

A TWA Boeing 707-331B on approach to the Frankfurt/Main airport. *Author's archive*

707-320B ADVANCED

This version of the 707-320 included all the aerodynamic improvements of the 707-320C, but without the cargo door and the two additional emergency exits aft of the wings.

707-320C

Combi or pure freight version of the 707-320B, with a large cargo door on the passenger deck in front of the wings. Reinforced cabin floor and undercarriage to accept the higher loads in cargo service.

A small emergency exit door was present on each side of the fuselage, near the wing trailing edge. These were necessary because the combined passenger-freight version's cargo hold was located in the forward fuselage, and the forward exits were thus not accessible to passengers in the event of an emergency. The 707-320C was built without the ventral fin beneath the tail.

707-400

Version of the 707-320B with Rolls-Royce Conway turbofan engines.

707-700

Single 707-320C built with CFM-56 turbofan engines for test purposes.

720

Lighter version of the 707-100 shortened by 8.8 ft., with modified wings and tail. Smaller ventral fin beneath the tail compared to the 707-100.

Equipped with high-lift Krueger flaps on the wing leading edges.

Thickening of the wing leading edge, the so-called wing glove modification, between the fuselage and inner engine pylons to raise maximum speed to Mach 0.906.

720B

New-production 720s powered by Pratt & Whitney JT3D turbofan engines, or older aircraft retrofitted with the new engines.

The horizontal stabilizers were each lengthened by 24 inches.

Note: The type designations shown in ascending model number have no chronological connection. For example, the first 707-400s and 720Bs flew before the 320B version.

SPOTLIGHT

In the twenty-four hours of October 22, 1962, the 273 Boeing 707 and 720 aircraft that had been delivered to airlines around the world logged 2,662 flying hours and covered a total of 1,108,930.7 miles. They carried 48,261 passengers and 757 metric tons of cargo and mail on a total of 769 flights all over the world. They flew to 146 cities in sixty countries and completed 1,952 takeoffs and landings.

Compare the numbers for the Lufthansa Boeing jet fleet: between March 17, 1960, and December 1962, it covered 27,340,332 miles in the course of 6,750 scheduled and charter flights. That was equivalent to 1,100 flights around the earth. In that period, the Lufthansa Boeing 707-430s and 720Bs carried 676,000 passengers plus 11,870 metric tons of freight and 3,201 metric tons of air mail.
Source: *Der Lufthanseat*, December 1962

Loading freight into a Boeing 707-320C of ZAS Airline of Egypt at Skavsta
Airport, south of Stockholm. *Author's archive*

"Family gathering" of Boeing 707s belonging to BOAC, TWA, and VARIG of Brazil
at New York's Idlewild Airport. The VARIG aircraft is a 707-441 with Rolls-Royce
Conway engines. *Jon Proctor*

Continental Airlines' Golden Jet livery looks particularly good on this Boeing
720B photographed at Los Angeles. *Jon Proctor*

CHAPTER 6
BLUEPRINT FOR MODERN CABIN DESIGN

UGLINESS DOES NOT SELL.

—Raymond Loewy, American design legend

Graphic depiction of the Lufthansa Boeing 707 jets from the early 1960s.
Author's archive

For seven decades, beginning with the Type 377 Stratocruiser, the US company Walter Dorwin Teague Associates (WDTA) has been responsible for the interior design of all Boeing passenger aircraft. After the luxurious bar in the Stratocruiser's lower deck, followed by the individual service modules under the overhead bins of the Boeing 707, to the futuristic cabin design of the Boeing 787 Dreamliner, Teague has repeatedly set trends in cabin design on behalf of Boeing over the past decades.

The list of protagonists involved in designing the cabin of the Boeing 707 reads like a Who's Who of the American design scene of the 1950s. First and foremost, there was the architect, illustrator, graphic and industrial designer, and entrepreneur Walter Dorwin Teague. From 1926 until 1960, he advised American companies on their product designs and was thus one of the fathers of modern "corporate design." Teague designed cameras for Kodak, came up with the design of Steinway concert grand pianos, defined the appearance of American long-distance trains and automobiles as well as Texaco gas stations, and became known to an international audience at the latest by designing pavilions at the New York World's Fair in 1939–40. To deal with a growing number of commissions and employees,

Walter Dorwin Teague Associates (WDTA) has designed the passenger cabins of all Boeing commercial airliners since the 1940s. This unique symbiosis between an aircraft maker and a design bureau continues to the present day. Shown here is the Teague-designed first-class lounge of an American Airlines Boeing 707. *Jon Proctor*

This photo of the economy-class cabin of a Lufthansa Boeing 707-430 from 1966 shows the comfortable layout of the passenger seats compared to the extremely narrow backrests and sparsely upholstered seat cushions common today. *Lufthansa*

In the mid-1970s the passenger cabins of the Lufthansa 707 fleet were given a "wide-body look" adapted to the prevailing taste of the time. This included new side panels in the style of the 747 jumbo jet and overhead luggage compartments. The photo was taken in 1975 and shows the first-class cabin of a 707-330B. *Lufthansa*

Teague founded the design firm Walter Dorwin Teague Associates in 1945. With the company founder as owner, later joined by his son Walter Dorwin Teague Jr., senior staff members were able to qualify for a WDTA partnership. Among these chosen "associates" was designer Frank Del Guidice, to whom Teague entrusted the establishment and management of the Seattle office, founded in 1946. Previously, WDTA had signed a contract with Boeing for the cabin design of what was probably the most luxurious passenger aircraft of its time—the Boeing 377 Stratocruiser. Neither Teague nor Boeing might have guessed at the time that this unique symbiosis between an external design firm and the world's leading aerospace company would continue to this day. Starting with the 377, Teague designed the passenger cabins for the Boeing 707, 720, 727, 727, 737, 747, 757, 767, 777, and 787. This included the ongoing adaptation of the individual cabins to continually evolving modern tastes.

While the interior of the Boeing 377 piston-engine airliner still borrowed design elements from the luxury compartments of famous American and European long-distance trains, Teague deliberately set new accents with the Boeing 707 as the first American passenger jet. This design was so successful that its basic features are still considered a blueprint for the cabin design of modern commercial aircraft.

From the outset, the 707 cabin was designed for maximum flexibility and optimum utilization of available floor space. This was ensured, for example, by seat benches that could be moved on rails to adjust spacing, and easily movable supply units arranged under the overhead luggage compartments. There were service devices above the passengers' heads, such as a call button for the cabin crew, fresh-air nozzles, loudspeakers, illuminated "No Smoking" and "Fasten Seat Belt" signs, reading lamps, and the obligatory oxygen masks for the "unlikely event." Also new were wall panels and partitions between the seating classes, made of easy-to-care-for PVC. Downright revolutionary, however, were the plastic screens on every window, which marked a departure from the living-room flair of the fabric curtains previously installed in the propeller planes, which were still present in the cabins of the competing Douglas DC-8 jetliner.

During the 707's design phase, Boeing had recognized in good time that the jet's higher productivity would lead to falling ticket prices in the medium term. Accordingly, the cabin windows were spaced 19.7 inches apart in order to provide passengers in tourist class, which was introduced over the North Atlantic in 1952, and whose seats were closer together, with a window seat. In contrast, the cabin windows of the Douglas DC-8 were placed 39.4 inches apart, which was in line with the first-class seat spacing in use by American Airlines at that time. In principle this was not an error, since at the time that the DC-8 project was launched in the mid-1950s, many airlines were in fact operating the newest flagships of their fleets exclusively with a luxurious first-class seating arrangement, preferring to use older aircraft for the cheaper tourist-class flights. By the time the Boeing 707 and Douglas DC-8 entered scheduled service, however, the jets were already flying with combined first-class and economy-class seating. This was the only way to fill the jet airliners, which were twice as large and twice as fast as the propeller airliners they replaced, and to operate them economically.

The new economy class was approved by the international airline umbrella organization IATA in 1958, just in time for the start of the jet age, and this meant the ability to offer fares on the new jets that were at least 20 percent lower than the original tourist-class fares of the propeller age.

TEST FLIGHTS IN A WAREHOUSE

The design of the Boeing 707 cabin presented by WDTA was so futuristic by the standards of the day that Boeing managers first wanted to get the opinion of potential customers and the professional public before they dared to make this radical break with all previously known interior designs. They therefore arranged to have a 100 ft. long "cabin flight simulator" built on the eighth floor of a New York warehouse. It was fully functional and thus created the illusion of a flight aboard the 707 as realistically as possible. To make the flight experience as true to life as possible, engine sounds and announcements by the captain were played from a tape recorder, and lamps positioned around the fuselage simulated the ever-changing daylight shining through the cabin windows at an altitude of 32,808 ft. The passengers invited by Boeing to take part in this special flight were served drinks and hot meals from the fully functional galleys by stewardesses and, if necessary, could use the likewise fully functioning washrooms. Incidentally, the flush toilet also made its air travel debut on board the Boeing 707!

Boeing had such high hopes for this mockup that the aircraft manufacturer was prepared to invest a tenth of the purchase price of a real 707 in its construction. After its completion in 1956, Boeing launched its virtual 707. After each "landing," passengers were asked for their opinion of the simulated flight and their individual impressions of the new cabin.

The insights gained in the process flowed directly into the final 707 cabin layout. At a time when the IATA cartel determined global fares, and airlines could compete only on the basis of the service they offered, the individual cabin layout of an airliner was of great importance. The basic concept designed by Teague was adapted to the specific wishes of each individual 707 customer. In addition to the basic modules offered by Boeing, such as first-class lounges, galleys, and passenger seats, the airlines were also able to take delivery of their brand-new aircraft in Renton without a complete cabin interior and then have this fitted as part of a "postdelivery modification" after the aircraft had been delivered to their respective home bases. In this case, the side panels, partition walls, galleys, and washrooms were preassembled by Boeing and adapted

The double-globe emblem designed by Raymond Loewy adorns the tail of this Boeing 707 of Trans World Airlines. *Dr. John Provan*

to the customer's design prior to handover. This procedure is still common practice at Boeing today, since it allows airlines to save the cost of transporting their cabin components to Seattle, avoid customs problems, and exclude the possibility of damage to the expensive cabin fittings from the outset. Other design luminaries left their mark on these customized 707 cabins. Among them was Henry Dreyfuss, who not only designed the color scheme for American's 707 and 720 cabins but also designed the

aircraft livery that launched American into the jet age. Like Walter Dorwin Teague and his son Walter Dorwin Teague Jr., who continued his father's legacy after his death, Henry Dreyfuss was already an icon of US industrial design before he was commissioned by American Airlines. His catalog of works ranges from vacuum cleaners, steam locomotives, public telephones, and tractors to oceangoing passenger liners.

Raymond Loewy designed the livery worn by the Air Force One VIP jets used by American presidents in consultation with President John F. Kennedy. The Boeing 707 (VC-137C) seen here on display at the Museum of Flight, near Seattle, was the first Air Force One painted in the livery designed by Loewy. *Jon Proctor*

THE BOEING 707 IN LUFTHANSA'S CHANGING LIVERY

This Boeing 707-430 wears the Lufthansa livery in use when it was
delivered to the airline in 1960. The livery was adapted from the one worn by
the airline's earlier propeller-driven airliners. *Lufthansa*

As a first adaptation of the design proposed by Otl Aicher in 1962, this 707-330, photographed at New York, bears the solid-blue side stripe, which replaced the blue-and-yellow parabola. *Lufthansa*

The designer Raymond Loewy, who is considered one of the fathers of American streamline design, also made a name for himself. His design of the American Greyhound intercity buses caused a sensation—but his best-known work is probably the packaging for Lucky Strike cigarettes, which are distributed all over the world. In keeping with his credo that "ugliness doesn't sell," in 1959 Loewy developed the "Star Stream" livery with its striking gold double-globe logo, which was introduced with the delivery of the first Boeing 707 to Trans World Airlines.

Loewy's reputation for excellence preceded him, and US president John Fitzgerald Kennedy commissioned him to design a special livery for the US Air Force's Boeing 707 (VC-137C) VIP jets, which were to use the legendary "Air Force One" call sign when the American president was on board. To this day, this design by Loewy remains the basis for the aircraft used by American presidents and other members of the government. Raymond Loewy paid one last honor to President Kennedy, who was assassinated in November 1963, by designing a commemorative stamp, which was issued by the US Postal Administration in 1964. Loewy, who created the first logo of the newly formed US Postal Service in 1971, is himself the subject of a commemorative stamp issued in 2011, twenty-five years after his death.

The dawning of the jet age motivated not only TWA but most airlines around the globe to introduce a new visual identity. While the era of the propeller-driven airliner, which ended in 1958, was characterized mostly by a lack of a uniform design concept in air travel, numerous airlines combined the commissioning of their new fast flagships with a uniform "corporate identity." The US airline Pan American (1928–1991), whose global route network covered all continents, was the leader, and not just in design matters. The airline commissioned the architects Edward Larabee Barnes and Charles Forberg to redesign the appearance of its Boeing 707-120. The result, displayed for the first time in the autumn of 1958, was a very modern-looking aircraft, even from today's perspective, which continued in this form until the 1980s. Other airlines, such as Deutsche Lufthansa, followed suit at the beginning of the 1960s and followed the Pan Am example not only with

In this photo, taken on the ramp at John F. Kennedy Airport in New York, the
Lufthansa lettering has been replaced by the Helvetica font preferred by
Aicher; however, the blue-and-yellow parabola is still present on the aircraft's
tail. *Jon Proctor*

After it was retired by Lufthansa, the cockpit of the former D-ABUF was updated with display screens. In this photo, some instruments have already been removed in preparation for the planned scrapping of this 707-330B. *Guy van Herbruggen*

Just before it was to be scrapped in early 2019, the former D-ABUF was resplendent in striking VIP jet livery. *Guy van Herbruggen*

The Boeing 707-330B in the Aicher-designed livery, which was revised once again in 1967 and remained in use until 1989. *Lufthansa*

The graphic stylistic elements developed by Otl Aicher in 1962 still characterize the visual appearance of Lufthansa. These flight schedules from 1966 and 1967 with their Boeing 707 silhouettes seem tirelessly modern. *Lufthansa*

a new aircraft livery, but a holistic appearance covering everything from the paper tickets to the onboard tableware to the painting of the aircraft stairs.

Lufthansa's Boeing 707s thus became the experimental canvas for the revolutionary design that Otl Aicher and Development Group 5 (E5) of the Academy of Design, which he headed, unveiled in 1962 as Lufthansa's new, holistic image. Thanks to Otl Aicher and the E5 Group, the principle of "corporate identity" celebrated its premiere not only at Lufthansa, but in Germany in general. The proposals made by Aicher, however, were a shade too revolutionary for the taste of Lufthansa's board of directors at the time. After all, the developers initially planned to paint the tail of the aircraft in a pale-yellow shade and to let the Lufthansa crane fly freely inside it. On a trial basis, the vertical stabilizer of the 707-430 D-ABOF was partially painted in the original Aicher look, but it was soon adapted to match the rest of the fleet, and its parabolic livery was carried over from the propeller era. It was not until 1967 that the Lufthansa design department prevailed with its revised design of a blue vertical tail with a blue crane logo on a yellow circle. This traditional livery, which was to stay with Lufthansa for twenty-two years until 1989, was thus finally born.

CHAPTER 7
POWER FOR THE
BOEING 707
TURBOJET AND TURBOFAN
POWER PLANTS

This patent, submitted by Joachim Pabst von Ohain, was the basis for jet propulsion. *Author's archive*

When the German airline's first Boeing 707-430 landed at the Fuhlsbüttel airport on March 2, 1960, Lufthansa warned its invited guests on the apron of its Hamburg base with instructions such as "Beware of Jet Blast" and "Danger Jet Intake." The jet age in air travel had now also begun in Germany—two years after the American competition, which had been flying their jet clippers between the United States and Europe since October 1958.

The jet age had celebrated its world premiere in Germany twenty-one years earlier. The He S 3 engine, developed by Hans-Joachim Pabst von Ohain at the Heinkel aircraft works, located at the mouth of the Warnow near Rostock, was a revolution. Parallel to the research work by the Englishman Frank Whittle, and without knowledge of his equally secret activity, von Ohain had built the world's first operational jet engine. On August 27, 1939, the Heinkel He 178 V1 experimental aircraft took off with Flugkapitän Erich Warsitz at the controls for the first test flight with the new jet engine, which would make possible previously

The Heinkel He 178 was the world's first jet-powered aircraft. It took to the air for the first time on August 27, 1939. *Author's archive*

The Heinkel He S 1 was the predevelopment stage of the He S 3 engine, which powered the Heinkel He 178. *Author's archive*

unheard-of speeds and altitudes. The jet age had irrevocably begun. Germany led the way in the development of jet engines and jet aircraft until the end of the Second World War. In addition to Heinkel, engine makers Junkers, Bramo, and BMW all researched and built turbojet engines, which were used in various types of aircraft such as the Arado 234, Messerschmitt Me 262, and Junkers 287.

The German aviation industry perished in the ruins of the Third Reich, and it was not until the nation regained air sovereignty in 1955 that it again gained momentum. The British aircraft maker de Havilland had the honor of becoming the first manufacturer to design not only a jetliner, which had been in development since 1943, but also its power plants. In July 1952, British Overseas Airways Corporation inaugurated the jet age in scheduled air traffic

The de Havilland Ghost turbine, power unit of the Comet mainliner, not only enjoys a basic advantage of efficiency through direct air entry but also offers unprecedented standards in simplicity, robustness, accessibility, fire prevention and ice protection. It follows in the tradition of the Gipsy.

with the de Havilland 106 Comet. Contemporaneous reports celebrated the smooth flight bestowed by the aircraft's four jet engines, far above the turbulent weather. The de Havilland Ghost engines that powered the Comet 1 were still equipped with a complex centrifugal-flow compressor. The aircraft that followed the Comet were powered exclusively by axial-flow engines, whose compressor stages were arranged on the central shaft one behind the other like a string of pearls.

A famous example of the axial-flow engine is the Pratt & Whitney J-57, which is considered the "forefather" of all modern engines for jet airliners. The first versions of the Boeing 707 were, like those of the competing Douglas DC-8, equipped with the JT3, the engine's civil variant. This was the only available American-made civil engine in the required power output range. It was a derivative of the military J-57 engine, which Boeing had already used to power its B-52 bomber. The JT3C was followed by the somewhat more powerful JT4A. A common feature of both engines was that they did not have the high bypass ratio common in modern engines. The British engine manufacturer Rolls-Royce took this significant evolutionary step with the world's first civil turbofan engine, the Rolls-Royce Conway. Its ducted fan made the turbofan engine more economical and quieter than pure turbojets.

Both Boeing and Douglas engineers feared that the early Pratt & Whitney JT3C and JT4A and Rolls-Royce Conway engines had leaky bearings, whose oil vapor might contaminate the cabin air and thus unsettle the passengers and crew. For this reason, both the Boeing 707 and the Douglas DC-8 were fitted with turbo-compressors, which built up the cabin pressure by compressing the ambient air. In the case of the 707, these compressors sat directly on the engine nacelles and could be recognized from the

The Comet 1's Ghost engine, produced by de Havilland, could not be developed further due to its centrifugal-flow design, and in Great Britain it gave way to the Rolls-Royce Avon axial-flow turbojet. *Dave Robinson collection*

The Boeing 707-123 Flagship Oklahoma during testing of its Pratt & Whitney engines at the Los Angeles airport in 1959. Only the relatively ancient-looking apron vehicle gives some idea when this image of the 707, which still looks modern today, was actually taken. *Bob Proctor*

Members of Lufthansa's technical department examine the Rolls-Royce Conway power plants of the first Boeing 707-430 following its arrival in Hamburg. *Author's archive*

This Rolls-Royce Conway engine is on display at the RAF Museum Cosford. *Wolfgang Borgmann*

The Boeing 720B was the first aircraft of the 707 family to be built with Pratt & Whitney JT3D high-bypass-ratio turbofan engines. *Boeing*

Apart from Lufthansa, for reasons of national prestige BOAC was the sole customer for the Boeing 707 with domestic Rolls-Royce engines. *Jon Proctor*

Checks on a Pratt & Whitney JT3C engine of a Trans World Airlines Boeing 707. Above the engine intake is the air intake for the turbo-compressor, which maintained cabin pressure. *ETH Zurich, Swissair*

front by the small air intakes above the actual engine. They were driven by compressed air from one of the engine's compressor stages, which did not come into contact with the breathing air for the cabin. Both the 707-120 and -420 were equipped with four turbo-compressors, but the 707-330B had only three, which sat on engines number 2, 3, and 4. Since, as we well know, there is an exception to every rule, not every engine pod had a compressor installed. Air India's 707-420s flew with two compressors and, for optical reasons, two more empty fairings, while American Airlines' 707-320B also had only two compressors installed, and only these had the distinctive sheet metal fairings. Finally, two compressors, which were installed on engines 2 and 3, were also sufficient for the Boeing 720. Lufthansa, whose Boeing customer number was thirty, became the first customer for the Conway-powered Boeing 707, which was now designated the 430 version. The American response followed soon afterward in the form of the Pratt JT3D turbofan engine, which became the standard power plant for all subsequent versions of the Boeing 707 and Douglas DC-8. This engine was based on the J-57 engine core, to which was added a two-stage fan with a bypass ratio of 1.43. The story of the JT3D is a typical episode of the time, when a manager's word was more important and counted for more than pages and pages of contracts. Startled by General Electric's announcement that it was going to develop an economical and powerful turbofan engine called the GE CJ-805-23 for the projected Convair 990, Boeing feared that this would negatively affect orders for its 707 and 720 jet models. Pratt & Whitney and Boeing decided to develop the JT3D engine over a few drinks on the fringes of an aviation conference held in January 1958. A few days later, the engine manufacturer was already presenting specific performance data—and the rest is history. Mainly due to the powerful Pratt & Whitney turbofan engine, the Boeing 707-320B and 720B proved superior to the CV 990 and pushed Convair out of the civil aircraft market.

In contrast to the competing Douglas DC-8-71, -72, and -73, Boeing failed to establish a sustainable civil program to equip a version of the 707 with the GE/Snecma CFM-56 turbofan engine. Only an experimental civil aircraft dubbed the 707-700 and a few military KC-135 variants were equipped with the engine, first offered for the Boeing 737-300 in the early 1980s, which for a time became the standard engine for the 737 and Airbus A320 families. The program offered by the "Seven Q Seven" consortium shortly after the turn of the millennium, to reengine the 707-320C with quieter, more-powerful, and more-fuel-efficient Pratt & Whitney JT8D-219 engines, also came to nothing. The company, based in San Antonio, Texas, initially had to suspend its certification program for the aircraft, marketed as the 707RE (which began in August 2001), after the September 11 attacks and was unable to win any military or civilian customers in the years that followed.

The Boeing 707 was designed to transport a spare engine in an aerodynamically shaped transport pod under the port wing. In this way, engines could be moved without great logistical effort between the individual destinations within an airline's route network. This photo, taken in 1969, shows one such transport, using the example of a Pan Am 707-321B landing at Los Angeles. *Terry Waddington*

This photo depicts a NASA McDonnell Douglas F-15 research aircraft refueling from a KC-135 retrofitted with CFM 56 turbofan engines. *NASA / Carla Thomas*

CHAPTER 8
FIRST CUSTOMER:
PAN AMERICAN
WORLD AIRWAYS
THE JETS FOR JUAN TRIPPE

The first order for the Boeing 707-120 was preceded by an unprecedented poker game between the airline on one side and the aircraft manufacturers Boeing and Douglas on the other. Lockheed president Gross, who had also been invited to bid, declined to participate in the Pan Am tender on the grounds that two comparable aircraft types would be sufficient to meet the expected demand. Juan Terry Trippe, who had founded what was then the most renowned airline in the world on October 28, 1928, at the age of twenty-eight, was at first the only airline boss to show interest in the four-jet designs by Boeing and Douglas. He thus held all the trump cards—and knew how to use them. The fate of the civil Boeing 707 project and of the Douglas DC-8 hung on his order. Despite the tragedy surrounding the British de Havilland Comet 1, Trippe clung to the idea of jet air travel. The Pan Am president had firm ideas about what his long-haul jet should look like. Douglas was the first manufacturer to be ready to develop its DC-8 base model around the new Pratt & Whitney J-75 (the later JT4 engine), in keeping with Pan Am's demands. If Boeing did not want

The Boeing 707-121 Jet Clipper Washington undergoes servicing at the Pan Am Worldport at New York Idlewild. The aircraft, with the registration N712PA, was later retrofitted with the larger tail and ventral stabilizer and turbofan engines. *Bob Proctor*

In September 1958, Pan Am invited employees and outside guests to inspect its first Boeing 707-121 inside Hangar 14 at New York's Idlewild Airport—one month prior to the type's maiden flight to Paris. The third 707 produced by Boeing bore the registration N709PA and the name "Clipper America." Five years later it was lost in tragic fashion after a lightning strike over Maryland that ignited the fuel-air mixture in an almost empty fuel tank. All eighty-one people on board perished in the accident. *Allan van Wickler*

Pan Am illustration of the Boeing 707's maiden flight from New York to Paris on October 26, 1958. *Author's archive*

Pan

American -

PAST

PRESENT

FUTURE . . .

to lose the lucrative contract to its Californian competitor, the aircraft maker from Seattle would have to improve its basic model. After long, tough negotiations, Boeing president Bill Allen finally agreed to supplement the 707-120 with the Pratt & Whitney JT3 engine, originally offered with a new model with a greater wingspan, a longer fuselage, increased range, and more-powerful JT-4 engines. The Boeing 707-320 Intercontinental was born. The most successful of all Boeing 707 variants was the result of Juan Trippe's perseverance.

Contrary to the official Pan Am chronicle, which describes this as the first order for jet aircraft by a US airline, it was in fact Pan Am's second attempt to enter the jet age. In 1952, Trippe had traveled to the de Havilland Aircraft Corporation at Hatfield, Great Britain, to place an order for three Comet 3s. But after the Comet program stalled in 1954, de Havilland withdrew its Comet 3s from the market, and Pan Am had to continue waiting for its first jet.

Pan Am had originally intended to enter the jet age with the de Havilland Comet 3, depicted in this photo of a model and the airline's brochure. After the Comet's certificate of airworthiness was withdrawn in April 1954 as a result of metal fatigue, Pan Am would have been forced to wait until the improved Comet 4 became available. Several of these aircraft were operated by Pan Am's subsidiary Mexicana. *Author's archive*

Pan American advertisement on board its Boeing 707s in the 1960s. The ad states that "Pan American offers experience of inestimable value . . . and excellent hot meals, even in Economy Class." *Author's archive*

Two generations of air transport meet at the Frankfurt airport. Just two decades of technological advancement in aircraft design separated the Douglas DC-3 and the Boeing 707. *Dr. John Provan*

1958: FLIGHT OPERATIONS BEGIN

Three years after its spectacular order placed with Boeing and Douglas, Pan Am was able to take off into the jet age over the North Atlantic—twenty-two days after the British airline BOAC, which won the race to make the first scheduled transatlantic commercial flight with the completely redesigned Comet 4. It was a belated success for de Havilland, but it was not enough to provide decisive impetus to the Comet program. Production of the airliner was halted in 1964 after twelve years and 113 aircraft delivered.

On October 26, 1958, Pan Am Boeing 707-120 "Jet Clipper America," with the registration N711PA, took off from New York for Paris on the type's first commercial flight. Pan Am had ordered six examples of this basic model of the 707, which would later be replaced on its North Atlantic routes by the better-performing Boeing 707-320. In addition to the smooth, quiet flight above the clouds, the passengers of Pan Am's jet service were also able to enjoy another innovation for the first time: economy class. Compared to tourist class, which had been introduced on propeller-driven airliners in 1952, economy class was at least 20 percent less expensive. Still—compared to what is offered by most airlines in 2019—spacing between rows was extremely generous, and the onboard service was opulent. Thanks to the Boeing 707, the aircraft was well on its way to establishing itself as a mode of mass transport and losing its image as an exclusive means of transport for the "rich and beautiful."

In 1959 a first-class return ticket between New York and London on Pan Am cost 783 American dollars. The same trip in economy class on the Boeing 707 was offered for 436 dollars, which, on the basis of the higher value of the American currency at the end of 2018, was equivalent to about 940 Euros. The new fares and the short flight times made the new long-range jet a popular alternative to the competing ocean liners. In the first three months of 1959, Pan Am's 707 fleet carried 33,400 passengers. And that was in its first year of operation, with almost no competition, since apart from the smaller Comet 4 flown by BOAC, there were no other jets in service on the North Atlantic routes. The reason: with its orders, Pan Am had blocked the Boeing 707 final-assembly line for almost a year. Since Douglas and its DC-8 program were a year behind the Boeing 707, the first examples of the competing Douglas DC-8-30 did not enter service on the North Atlantic route until 1960, including with KLM, SAS, and Swissair.

EARLY START FOR THE JETS

On both sides of the Atlantic, after the Pan Am order the leading airlines found themselves forced to prematurely withdraw their still relatively new piston-engine airliners from service and replace them with jets. The danger of losing market share to the faster and more comfortable—but initially much too large—jet aircraft flown by the competition was too great. For most airlines, therefore, the beginning of the jet age came at the worst possible time. While the latest generation of propeller airliners such as the Douglas DC-7C and Lockheed L-1649 Starliner had entered service only in the mid-1950s, also purchasing new jetliners put an unplanned strain on the airlines' balance sheets. The airline managers could already foresee that the long-haul aircraft with piston engines that had just been delivered would soon be taken out of service—and thus dramatically depreciate in value—long before the date originally calculated by the accountants.

This photograph was taken on November 22, 1971, eight years to the day after the assassination of President John F. Kennedy, in whose honor New York Idlewild Airport was posthumously renamed. The Boeing 707-321B with the registration N881PA, shown here, wears the abbreviated Pan Am logo of the 1970s, which replaced the longer Pan American logo of the previous decade. *Jon Proctor*

CHAPTER 9
LUFTHANSA:
OPERATION PAPER JET

THE POWER OF THE ENGINES AND THE ENTIRE SIZE OF THE MACHINE CREATE THE IMPRESSION OF CONTROLLING A HUGE INDUSTRIAL PLANT WITH JUST A FEW LIGHT TOUCHES ON A COMPUTER.

—Lufthansa captain and member of the board Werner Utter about the change from the Lockheed Super Constellation to the Boeing 707

A member of the Operation Paper Jet team calculating the optimal routes of flight over the North Atlantic. *Lufthansa*

The manufacturers of the first jetliners were not the only ones who ventured into unknown territory with the technical design of their jetliners. With no experience in operating commercial aircraft that were twice as fast and flew about twice as high as the piston-engine airliners used to date, the first customers for the jets also entered completely new territory. This circle included Lufthansa, whose first Boeing 707-430s were used primarily on the Frankfurt–New York route over the North Atlantic beginning March 1960, using the flight number LH 420. To be optimally prepared for the start of jet operations, the Federal Ministry of Transport initiated a study by the German Meteorological Service, the Federal Institute for Air Navigation Services (BFS), and Lufthansa under the code name "Operation Paper Jet."

Four years before the first flight of the intercontinental jet, Lufthansa's aim was to simulate Boeing 707-430 flights between Frankfurt and New York, which would have a significant influence on the operation of the jets. On the basis of the knowledge gained, the project partners defined optimal flight procedures and routes before the actual start

The first design study for the Lufthansa 707 published by Boeing had little in common with the actual livery worn by the aircraft. *Boeing*

The findings of Operation Paper Jet were evaluated and, collected in numerous folders, waited to be used in actual flight operations, which for Lufthansa began on March 17, 1960, with its first flight to New York. *Lufthansa*

of flight operations. While this was taking place, planning for the equipment, ground handling, maintenance, overhaul, and personnel training of the Lufthansa staff was also in full swing. Nothing would be left to chance!

Half a year prior to the start of Operation Paper Jet, whose virtual "maiden flight" left Frankfurt on November 5, 1956, the Special North Atlantic Regional Air Navigation Meeting of the International Civil Aviation Organization (ICAO) was held in Paris. Its aim was to set meteorological standards for the new jet flight altitudes. To this day, ICAO, as a suborganization of the United Nations, sets binding operational and technical standards for civil aviation around the globe. At the time, there was a need for haste, because with the de Havilland D.H. 106 Comet 4 of the British Overseas Airways Corporation (BOAC) and Pan American's Boeing 707-123, the first scheduled jet services across the North Atlantic were set to begin as early as autumn 1958. In February 1956, the ICAO members agreed to provide altitude weather charts, initially up to 30,000 ft. and thus at the expected flying altitudes of long-haul jet airliners.

The German Weather Service in Frankfurt went one step further and produced weather charts for each flight of a "paper jet" for the usual jet flight altitudes between 30,000 and 40,000 ft. These were based on the "0300 Zulu" (Greenwich Mean Time) reports from the altitude weather stations in the Northern Hemisphere. The resulting maps were used to determine strong wind currents at jet-cruising altitude, so-called jet streams. These bands of strong winds, which rotate in an easterly direction in the Northern Hemisphere, can reach velocities of up to 310 mph and can significantly lengthen westbound flight times and shorten them for flights in the opposite direction. Jet streams usually occur between the troposphere and stratosphere at typical jet-cruising altitudes and are caused by the collision of cooler masses of air from the polar region in the north and warmer air from the south. However, at present this natural engine of the jet stream is steadily weakening as a result of climate change.

Calculations made at that time also included temperature values at different flight altitudes as a further meteorological component, since these affected the performance of jet engines. The German Weather Service transmitted the received data to the aviation meteorological technicians at the Lufthansa hubs in Hamburg and Frankfurt and the Technical Planning and Flight Service Consulting departments of Deutsche Lufthansa.

In addition to weather data, what was then the Federal Office of Air Navigation Services (now DFS) provided information on traffic density on the planned flight routes, as well as at the destination airport, New York Idlewild, and the alternate airport, Boston. The aircraft performance data for the virtual flights were taken from the flight trials of the Boeing Dash 80 prototype.

This mountain of analog data—computers did not yet exist at that time—was supplemented by estimated passenger and freight figures as well as the expected flight profile, fuel consumption figures, and flight path of the simulated Boeing 707-430. More than 2,000 "Paper Jet" flights were completed by Lufthansa between November 1956 and March 1959 as part of the program, which was expanded in 1958 to include additional destinations in North America and the Paris–Dakar route over the South Atlantic. Lufthansa was thus well prepared for the weather conditions to be expected when the first Boeing intercontinental jet took off from Frankfurt for its scheduled flight to New York on March 17, 1960.

Station personnel such as the team from the Lufthansa station at the Hamburg airport, seen here, were also prepared for the beginning of jet operations. On the wall behind the counter are Lufthansa posters advertising its new Boeing intercontinental jet. *Ute Borgmann*

At the Hamburg training center, employees practice check-in by Lufthansa 707 passengers at special "jet counters," which were installed at the Frankfurt airport when the 707 entered service. *Lufthansa*

CHAPTER 10
LUFTHANSA: TAKEOFF INTO THE JET AGE WITH THE 707 INTERCONTI-NENTAL JET

WHEN EVERYTHING WORKED, IT FLEW LIKE A SPORTS PLANE.
—Didi Krauss, former Lufthansa 707 pilot.

When the age of long-haul jets began toward the end of the 1950s, there were three competing designs: the British de Havilland Comet 4, the Douglas DC-8 (built at Long Beach, California), and the 707 (produced by Boeing in Seattle). In 1957, Lufthansa decided on the Boeing 707 as the aircraft type best suited to its needs, initially ordering four of them. On March 17, 1960, it inaugurated jet service between Germany and New York with its first Boeing intercontinental jet.

The Boeing 707, 720B, 727, 737, 747, and 777—the aircraft types from Seattle—were and are an essential part of the Lufthansa fleet. Not only have almost six decades passed since the first scheduled flight by a Boeing 707 in Lufthansa's livery, but a close, trusting partnership has developed between the German airline and the American aircraft manufacturer with its German roots. Lufthansa, which has earned an excellent technical reputation since

Rollout of the first Lufthansa Boeing 707-430, with the registration D-ABOB,
at the Boeing factory at Renton, near Seattle. *Author's archive*

D-ABOB's arrival at Hamburg-Fuhlsbüttel on March 2, 1960, after the delivery flight from Renton. *Lufthansa*

Training prospective 707 pilots in a Link trainer at the Boeing factory. *Boeing*

its founding, provided Boeing with decisive input on various design features from the customer's point of view that finally turned a good concept into an outstanding aircraft design. This unique symbiosis continues to pay off for both companies today, since Boeing sells more aircraft as a result, while Lufthansa receives a tailor-made product.

The howl of factory sirens at the Lufthansa base in Hamburg joined that of the four Rolls-Royce Conway engines of the Boeing 707-430 on March 2, 1960, when the new flagship of the fleet touched down on the runway of the northern German airport at 11:51 a.m. At the controls of the aircraft, registered D-ABOB, were Lufthansa chief pilot Rudolf Mayr and Flugkapitän Werner Utter, who flew the route from Boeing Field in Renton, near Seattle, to the international airport of the Hanseatic city in exactly nine hours and forty-seven minutes. What happened after the landing on the apron of the Hamburg airport is described in an article in the Lufthansa employee magazine *Der Lufthanseat* from the year 1960: "The curiosity to see the inside this marvelous bird overpowered the crowd as it literally stormed the aircraft on the heels of the cleaning ladies. The station manager had to use all his powers of persuasion to get the motley crowd out again, a task made all the more difficult when the more than a hundred who had entered at the front collided with the hundred who had boarded the plane through the rear entrance."

The decision on which long-haul passenger jet to acquire as its first was not an easy one for Lufthansa. The choice lay between the Boeing 707 and the Douglas DC-8, aircraft types that were very similar in their dimensions and performance data. Having purchased the four-engine, propeller-driven Lockheed L1049G Super Constellation aircraft for intercontinental routes, Lufthansa found itself in a neutral position and favored neither Boeing nor the competing aircraft in the upcoming selection. This was in contrast to other European airlines such as Alitalia, KLM, SAS, and Swissair, which had already acquired Douglas DC-6 and DC-7 propeller-driven aircraft, and all gave preference to the DC-8. Lufthansa found itself in good company with other Lockheed Super Constellation

The Boeing 707 bearing the registration D-ABOC was the first aircraft of the new Lufthansa to be named. The photo shows Willy Brandt, then mayor of Berlin, christening the aircraft at Frankfurt. Lufthansa was not permitted to fly to Berlin until after reunification in 1989. *Lufthansa*

The Passenger Service Units common in all modern-day airliners were a special feature of the 707 cabin. They contained reading lamps, oxygen masks, and fresh-air nozzles. Easily relocated above the individual rows, they enabled flexible seating. *Lufthansa*

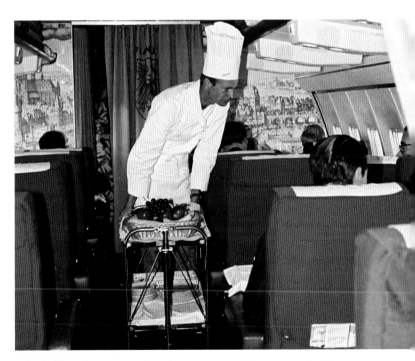

When Lufthansa's 707s entered service, passenger seats were covered with a red fabric. Historical motifs of their sponsor cities decorated the walls separating the cabins. *Lufthansa*

customers, such as Air France, BOAC, and Sabena, who also took a rather unbiased view—and acquired the Boeing 707.

Professor Ernst Simon was significantly involved in the company's internal decision-making processes in choosing between the Boeing 707 and Douglas DC-8. In a conversation that the author of this book had with him in 2013, he recalled: "We had taken great pains in the selection process and found that the Boeing 707 was by far the better and more advanced aircraft. At that time, Boeing, having produced the B-47 and B-52, had a very good team for the development of high-speed aircraft. The machines all had 35 degrees of wing sweep, based on research materials captured in Germany in 1945. These wings were very elastic and economical in cruising flight. The 707 was also more comfortable for the passenger, since its windows were installed 19.7 inches apart. Douglas had installed them the 'old-fashioned way,' separated by a distance of 39.4 inches. With varying seat spacing, some passengers on the DC-8 found themselves sitting in front of a blank wall and not at a window! We were also impressed by the 'Passenger Service Units,' in which the reading lights, oxygen masks, and fresh-air nozzles were housed. They could be variably arranged above the seats, thus allowing flexible seating."

Professor Simon had a personal influence on the selection of the most suitable engine for Lufthansa's new 707. This project, with which he was entrusted in 1956, was the first major independent task he had taken on for the Lufthansa Group. Lufthansa had indeed selected the

PROFESSOR ERNST SIMON

On March 30, 2014, Professor Ernst Simon died at the age of ninety-two. With him, the aviation world lost a highly esteemed expert in the field of civil aviation, whose incomparable competence was in demand far beyond Lufthansa until the time of his death. For many years, from 1953 until his retirement in 1986, Professor Ernst Simon was head of the technical projects department in the Lufthansa Engineering Directorate and in that capacity was responsible for the evaluation and selection of new Lufthansa aircraft types.

Boeing 707 as its first long-haul jet in February of that year, but at that time it had not yet decided on which engine would power the aircraft. Two engines were available: the JT4A offered by Pratt & Whitney as the standard power plant for the first 707, whose military version, the J-75, had already been tested, and the completely new Conway developed by the British engine manufacturer Rolls-Royce. Lufthansa's chief technical officer, Gerhard Höltje, did not take the decision between these two models lightly and commissioned his three leading engineers to weigh well-founded pros and cons. The technical project manager and later Lufthansa executive board member Hans Süssenguth, the head of the Power Plant Engineering Department and later technical director Heinz Kressner, and junior engineer Ernst Simon were given the task of making their personal recommendations. Only Ernst Simon courageously spoke out in favor of the more advanced Rolls-Royce engine. This engine, the first civilian turbofan engine with a modest bypass ratio of 0.4, was about 2 tons lighter than the competing American model and consumed 2 percent less fuel. But all this was only theoretical at the time. Höltje relied on Ernst Simon's vote, and Lufthansa became the launch customer for the Rolls-Royce Conway—even before the British airline BOAC.

The first example of the Boeing 707-430 left the Boeing 707 final-assembly line in Renton, near Seattle, in January 1960. Flugkapitän Werner Utter, who was appointed to the Lufthansa executive board a good ten years later, on November 1, 1972, selected Tucson airfield in the state of

Arizona as a suitable location for training Lufthansa's future 707 pilots. To the present day, Lufthansa flight students and pilots are trained in favorable meteorological and climatic conditions at Lufthansa Aviation Training's Airline Training Center in Phoenix, Arizona, in preparation for service in the airline's cockpits.

A field report describes the experiences of the first 707 crews during flight training in Tucson: "Maneuvering the 707-430 on the ground presents no difficulties at all. Takeoff characteristics—even at simulated maximum takeoff weight—are good when the prescribed procedures are followed. Failure of an outboard engine during the takeoff procedure shortly after reaching V_1 requires the utmost concentration and promptest reaction on the part of the pilot. However, the 707-430 can be flown perfectly if the prescribed procedures are strictly adhered to. It is to be expected that a significant improvement will occur after the installation of 'full rudder boost.' The B707-430's climbing and maneuvering abilities are good even if one engine fails. As with any retraining on a new aircraft type, all flight conditions were experienced in the air. Low-speed flight characteristics (5 knots above stall speed) are surprisingly good, even at 30 degrees of bank. In contrast, the B707-430 can be flown perfectly at Vne (the maximum airspeed the aircraft should ever be operated at in smooth air). During training, special attention was paid to the characteristics of the B707-430 in a 'Dutch roll.' If handled correctly, no difficulties arise in the event of a 'Dutch roll,' be it at high altitude (40,000 ft.) or during takeoff and landing. Landing the B707-430 requires a completely different technique than that used until now. The pilot must strictly adhere to the speeds prescribed in the book, which depend on weight and flap position. Landings were carried out under difficult conditions, i.e., 3-engine landings or the failure of two engines on the same side. Landings were also carried out with the horizontal stabilizer locked, failed rudder boost, and without flaps, whereby in the latter case touchdown was dispensed with because of the high tire wear to be expected due to the high speed."

The commercial debut of the Lufthansa 707 followed on March 17, 1960, with the flight from Hamburg, via Frankfurt/Main, to New York. But the LH 420A route, offered only in March 1960, was dogged by bad luck. The Boeing intercontinental jet finally landed at what is now John F. Kennedy Airport seven hours and thirty-two minutes late. Technical problems and bad weather over the North Atlantic, which necessitated a diversion to Gander Airport in Newfoundland, were the reasons for this botched premiere. The return flight was not spared from mishaps either, since the dishes for Lufthansa's "Boeing service" were still well locked up in the New York customs warehouse. The plates and cups from the outbound flight therefore had to be washed before they could be reloaded for the guests on the return flight on D-ABOB.

The Boeing intercontinental jet with the registration D-ABOB in the foreground is parked next to its "little sister," the Boeing 720B D-ABOL. *Lufthansa*

Flying first class in 1965 was certainly no more comfortable than when the book was published, but the flying public clearly had more class in those days. Traveling in style was a matter of good manners back then, and not just in first class. *Lufthansa*

Nine years after the Boeing 707 entered service on April 1, 1955, the ten millionth Lufthansa passenger leaves one of the airline's 707s at the Stuttgart airport in June 1964. *Lufthansa*

D-ABOB, which was later christened "Hamburg," was the first aircraft in a series of a total of twenty-three Boeing 707s that Lufthansa ordered in three versions over the years. The new long-haul jets quickly replaced the slower Lockheed propeller-driven aircraft on the national carrier's global route network. And something else changed with the arrival of the jets at Lufthansa. Frankfurt/Main quickly took over from Hamburg as the starting point for overseas routes, thus manifesting its role as Lufthansa's largest hub, which it remains to this day.

In the case of flight LH 420, it took less than two weeks until the route was changed to Frankfurt to New York on April 1, 1960, and the Hanseatic city lost its Lufthansa overseas flight. The stationing of the 707 fleet in Frankfurt was accompanied by the establishment of a Lufthansa maintenance base at the Rhein-Main airport. This is how the largest aircraft maintenance hangar in the world—also known as the "butterfly hangar" because of its striking architecture—came to be built there in 1960. Lufthansa's technical base in Hamburg continued to be responsible for repairing and overhauling the Boeing fleet.

In 1960–61, the "crane airline" initially took delivery of five 707-430s with the Rolls-Royce Conway Mark 508 engines favored by Ernst Simon, which, as described above, were not only lighter and more economical than the alternative Pratt & Whitney JT4A-3 engines, but also somewhat quieter than the US power plants—if one can even speak of "quiet" in this context. From 1963 onward, these were followed by twelve Boeing 707-330Bs and six 707-330C freighters powered by considerably more-powerful Pratt & Whitney JT3D-3B engines. They made very long nonstop flights possible for the first time; for example, from Frankfurt to the West Coast of the United States.

In July 1961, his recommendation for the purchase of Boeing 707-330Bs with Pratt & Whitney JT3D engines and his preference for an order for additional Boeing 707-430s brought Professor Ernst Simon, head of the Hamburg Technical Projects Department, to Werner

Flugkapitän Werner Utter was copilot on the first Lufthansa Boeing 707 when it was flown from Seattle to Hamburg in March 1960, and entertained the passengers on the penultimate special flight to mark the retirement of the 707 at Lufthansa with his memories from twenty-four years of Boeing jets in service with the German airline. *Lufthansa*

Busch, then head of the Finance and Accounting Department at Lufthansa's Cologne headquarters, to explain himself. The latter demanded "auditable documents" from Simon to justify his recommendation to buy the further-developed Boeing intercontinental jet. Simon did not take long to explain, and he gave not one but five detailed reasons for his choice. These were the 330's significantly lower fuel consumption, greater range and higher payload on extreme long-distance routes, shared technology with the 707-330C freighters intended for Lufthansa Cargo, and commonality of engines with the Boeing 720B, as well as "long-term considerations," such as the possible procurement of further 707s by 1970, which for competitive reasons alone should be the technically and economically more advanced 707-330Bs. As Simon summarized, it was not a question of "Do we want to equip our 707s with

Rolls-Royce Conway or Pratt & Whitney JT3D engines, but rather that the Boeing 330B represents an improved model compared to the 430, which will not be delivered with Conway engines."

The last Boeing 707 delivered to Lufthansa was a freighter version of the type 707-330C with the registration D-ABUY and the name "Essen." As predicted by Professor Simon nine years earlier, it arrived in Germany on October 16, 1970.

INTO THE BLACK WITH BOEING JETS

In 1961, Lufthansa, like most other airlines, was struggling with overcapacities in world air traffic. Supply was running far ahead of actual demand. The revaluation of the deutsch mark as a result of the German economic miracle

Professor Ernst Simon had many good reasons for choosing the further-developed 707-320B instead of ordering more 707-430s with Rolls-Royce Conway engines. *Lufthansa*

also weighed on the airline's earnings, whose costs were incurred mainly in US dollars. Three more loss-making business years passed until Lufthansa finally reaped the fruits of its farsighted fleet policy in 1964. The investment in more-profitable jet aircraft was reflected for the first time in an eight-digit profit of 36,900,000 deutsch marks. The forty-two aircraft with the crane symbol on the tail carried more than 2.5 million passengers in 1964. In the same year, a Lufthansa aircraft took off and landed on the airline's global route network every 3.5 minutes on average. And yet another milestone was reached in June 1964: spurred by the big Boeing jets, at Stuttgart Deutsche Lufthansa welcomed its ten millionth passenger since the start of flight operations on April 1, 1955.

The Boeing 720B, a smaller and lighter version of the 707, with just 125 seats, made a major contribution to this success. On January 30, 1960, Lufthansa became the first European airline to purchase four of these aircraft equipped with new Pratt & Whitney JT3D-3 turbofan engines. After delivery of the first 720B on March 8, 1961, it operated eight of these very fast aircraft on medium- and long-haul routes. Lufthansa Boeing 720Bs were to be found at European and South American airports as well as on its African and Asian route network. In 1962, a Lufthansa aircraft covered the 1,891-mile route between Hong Kong and Tokyo in two hours and thirty-nine minutes. Its ground speed: 713 mph.

The 720B's flight performance was outstanding. Equipped with the same engines as its larger and heavier sister the 707-330, the agile 720B was very popular with Lufthansa pilots.

But as popular as it was, the 720B's service career with Lufthansa was a brief one, because the era of the Boeing

The Boeing 707 certainly did not look like a design from the 1950s, even when Lufthansa retired its fleet at the beginning of the 1980s. *Lufthansa*

727, which was more economical and lighter and had just three engines, began on medium-haul routes in 1964. On long-haul routes the passenger and freight volumes had developed so well that it became necessary to switch to the larger 707-330. At the end of 1965, Lufthansa finally closed the 720B chapter with the retirement of the last aircraft of this type in exchange for brand-new 707-330Bs.

On New Year's Eve 1984, the Boeing 707 era at Lufthansa came to an end with a farewell flight organized by employees. The 707 fleet had performed impressively for Lufthansa. For example, the freighter with the registration D-ABUA had covered a distance equivalent to that from Earth to the planet Mars in 75,000 flying hours. The most advanced long-range aircraft of its time when it entered service in 1960, two decades later technological progress had caught up with the 707. Last but not least, it was excessively high noise and fuel consumption figures that argued for its retirement.

German Cargo Services began operations as a Lufthansa subsidiary on March 10, 1977. It used its curry-colored 707-330Cs on worldwide ad hoc cargo flights until 1985. *Lufthansa*

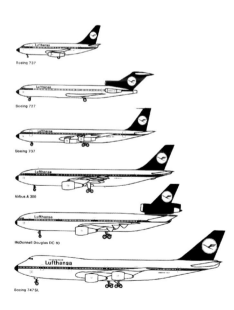

In 1979, the Lufthansa fleet included Boeing 707-330B passenger aircraft and 707-330C freighters. *Lufthansa*

The communications antenna on the tip of the vertical tail was an unmistakable recognition feature of the 707 and 720B jets. *Lufthansa*

LUFTHANSA BOEING 707 AND 720B HIGHLIGHTS

January 23, 1957
Boeing and Lufthansa sign a sales contract for four Boeing 707s as the first jet type for the airline founded four years earlier.

January 25, 1960
Lufthansa accepts its first Boeing 707-430, with the registration D-ABOB, at Seattle.

January 30, 1960
Lufthansa places an initial order for four Boeing 720Bs.

March 17, 1960
Lufthansa takes off into the jet age, initially making press flights from Hamburg via Frankfurt to New York Idlewild.

March 29, 1960
Opening of the "butterfly hangar," so called because of its shape, at the Frankfurt airport, built for the servicing of the airline's Boeing jets.

April 1, 1960
Beginning of daily scheduled service on the Frankfurt–New York route.

April 9, 1960
Lufthansa sets a new speed record, six hours and twenty-one minutes, on the Frankfurt–New York route. Average ground speed was 622 mph.

May 13, 1960
The Boeing 707-430 replaces the Lockheed 1049G on the Frankfurt–Chicago route. San Francisco is added as the third jet destination.

September 16, 1960
First naming of an aircraft by the postwar Lufthansa. Boeing 707-430 D-ABOC is christened "Berlin" by Willy Brandt, then mayor of Berlin and later chancellor of West Germany, at the Frankfurt airport. The aircraft was christened at Frankfurt because only the Western allies had been granted the privilege of flying to the western sector of Berlin. This restriction remained in place until German reunification in 1990.

January 23, 1961
The Boeing 707 replaces the Lockheed Super Constellation on the Far East route via Bangkok and Hong Kong to Tokyo.

March 8, 1961
Lufthansa takes delivery of its first Boeing 720B, with the registration D-ABOH.

May 5, 1961
Approximately 700 guests gather at the Cologne/Bonn airport for the christening of Lufthansa's first Boeing 720B, registration D-ABOH, with the name "Köln" (Cologne).

May 20, 1961
First scheduled flight by a Lufthansa Boeing 720B.

July 1, 1961
Boeing 720Bs take over the routes in the Near and Middle East from the propeller-driven aircraft previously used.

December 4, 1961
The Boeing 720B with the registration D-ABOK crashes while on a technical acceptance flight. All three crew members are killed.

March 4, 1962
The Boeing route to Lagos opens Lufthansa's "Africa Year," followed by links to Khartoum, Nairobi, and Johannesburg.

May 28, 1964
For the first time, a Lufthansa Boeing 707 flies the Frankfurt–Hamburg–Copenhagen–Fairbanks–Tokyo route over the North Pole. Beginning in September, Anchorage replaces Fairbanks on the route network.

July 15, 1964
The Boeing 720B with the registration D-ABOP crashes during a training flight. All three crew members are killed.

December 1964
Thanks in part to its economic jets, Lufthansa succeeds in presenting a positive annual result for the first time since its founding in 1953, with a profit of 36.9 million deutsch marks.

April 3, 1965
Lufthansa flies to the fifth continent for the first time. Depending on bookings, both the Boeing 707 and 720B are used on the Frankfurt–Athens–Karachi–Bangkok–Singapore–Darwin–Sydney route.

July 23, 1965
A baby girl enters the world aboard a Lufthansa Boeing 707 on the flight from Frankfurt to New York. In view of the unusual delivery room, the child's parents give her the name Barbara Lufthansa.

November 10, 1965
Lufthansa takes delivery of its first 707-330C freighter.

End of 1965
Lufthansa retires its last Boeing 720B.

December 19, 1973
The crew of Boeing 707-330B Duisburg makes a crash landing at Delhi. Although the aircraft is consumed by fire, all 109 persons on board manage to escape within ninety seconds.

March 10, 1977
Lufthansa establishes German Cargo Services GmbH for charter cargo flights and transfers some of its Boeing 707-330 freighter fleet to its new subsidiary. The aircraft are finished in a striking curry-color livery.

July 26, 1979
Boeing 707-330C D-ABUY Essen crashers near Rio de Janeiro, killing the three crew members on board. The accident was caused by an error on the part of local air traffic control.

May 25, 1984
Last scheduled flight by a Boeing 707 (D-ABUV) in Lufthansa colors.

December 31, 1984
Lufthansa bids farewell to its last Boeing 707 with a flight initiated by employees of the airline.

Not until July 1985 did the Lufthansa Group retire its last Boeing 707-330C, when German Cargo Services replaced its last Boeing freighter with a Douglas DC-8-73.

FLEET LIST

LUFTHANSA 707 AND 720

707-430

D-ABOB Hamburg
D-ABOC Berlin*
D-ABOD Frankfurt am Main
D-ABOF München (Munich)*
D-ABOG Bonn

707-330B

D-ABOV Berlin/Duisburg
D-ABOT Düsseldorf
D-ABOX Köln (Cologne)
D-ABUB Stuttgart
D-ABUC Bremen
D-ABUD Nürnberg (Nuremberg)
D-ABUF Hannover*
D-ABUG Essen*
D-ABUH Dortmund
D-ABUK Bochum
D-ABUL Duisburg
D-ABUM Bremen / Hanseatic Tours

707-330C

D-ABUA Europa/America
D-ABUE America
D-ABUI Asia
D-ABUJ Africa*
D-ABUO Australia
D-ABUY Essen

Boeing 720B

D-ABOH Köln (Cologne)
D-ABOK Düsseldorf
D-ABOL Stuttgart
D-ABOM Nürnberg (Nuremberg)
D-ABON Hannover
D-ABOP Bremen
D-ABOQ Essen
D-ABOR Dortmund

* Also used as passenger jet in service with Condor Flugdienst.

D-ABOS was a fictitious registration—used only in appropriately edited Lufthansa advertising photos and postcards distributed by the airline on its aircraft—for the Boeing 707-330B. In reality, no Lufthansa Boeing jet flew with this registration. *Lufthansa*

CHAPTER 11
LUFTHANSA: 707
SENATOR SERVICE

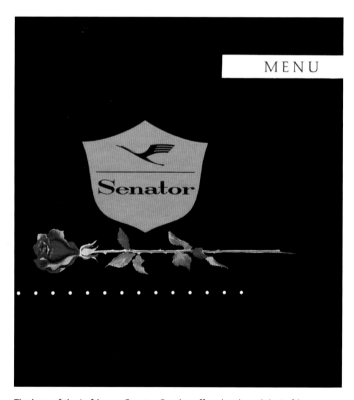

The logo of the Lufthansa Senator Service offered on board the Lufthansa Boeing 707 fleet. *Lufthansa*

As it had on the Lockheed Super Constellation and Super Star propeller-driven airliners, Lufthansa also offered its legendary Senator First Class Service on board its Boeing 707 intercontinental jets. A maximum of twenty-four first-class passengers were looked after by a hostess, a *chef de cabine*, and a chef steward. Berlin fashion designer Oestergard had specially designed a fashion collection "whose elegant and sporty lines pleasantly remind the passenger that he is on board the most modern and fastest aircraft in commercial aviation," says a Lufthansa paper from the year 1960. Starting with the 1960–61 winter flight schedule, the first foreign Lufthansa stewardesses began greeting passengers on board the 707 in order to respond to the individual wishes of passengers of different nationalities. Lufthansa continues this tradition to the present day with flight attendants of various nationalities on its flights.

The VIP Senator Service on board the Boeing 707 was not limited to obliging, attractively dressed crew, however. Beginning on November 1, 1960, a "bar lounge" designed and built by Lufthansa technicians was a convivial meeting place for well-heeled first-class passengers to have a drink above the clouds. It consisted of a standing bar with a

Jedes Flugzeug besitzt seine persönliche Note, unterscheidet sich irgendwie von dem anderen. Und doch werden Sie feststellen, daß alle eines gemeinsam haben: Für jeden Typ, auf jeder Strecke treffen die Worte zu: „LUFTHANSA führend im Service an Bord."

Each aircraft type has a character of its own and is somewhat different from the other according to operational requirements, — however, you will find that all aircraft have one thing in common: "LUFTHANSA is leading in Service on board".

Chaque avion a une note personnelle qui le différe des autres. Cependant, vous constaterez qu'ils ont tous quelque chose en commun: Pour chaque type d'avion, sur chaque ligne, une seule phrase est valable: LUFTHANSA en tête pour le service à bord.

LUFTHAN
1961
BOEING Jet

Lagos
Accra
Khartum
Nairobi
Salesbury
Johannesburg

Ankara
Athen
Baghdad
Bangkok
Barcelona
(Berlin)
Beyrouth
Bonn

Bremen
Buenos Aires
Cairo
Calcutta
Chicago
Dakar
Dhahran
Düsseldorf

Frankfurt
Genf
Hamburg
Hannover
Istanbul
Karachi
Kopenhagen

Köln
London
Madrid
Manchester
Milano
Montevideo
Montreal
München

New York
Nizza
Nürnberg
Paris
Rio de Janeiro
Rom
Santiago de Chile
São Paulo

Sao Fra
Stockho
Stuttga
Teherar
Tokyo
Wien
Zürich

The Boeing 707's exclusive onboard bar was a meeting place above the clouds for Lufthansa Senator first-class passengers. *Lufthansa*

The Senator bar on the 707-430 included a small lounge that was developed and built by Lufthansa technicians in the Hamburg workshops. *Lufthansa*

High proof was one way to pass the flight time on board. Lufthansa's 707s had neither film nor audio programs with which to distract the passengers. *Lufthansa*

Freshly tapped draft beer was one of the highlights of Lufthansa's Senator First Class Service on board the Boeing 707. *Lufthansa*

So-called chef stewards were responsible for preparing the meals in the galley and their presentation on the serving carts. Their distinguishing mark was the white chef's outfit, complete with imposing chef's hat. *Lufthansa*

Like their guests, the cabin crew on board Lufthansa Boeing 707s were very elegantly dressed. *Lufthansa*

bottle carousel, two double bench seats facing each other, and all sorts of accessories such as lighting, carpets, and side panels. Lufthansa first tested the design of each of its "bar lounges," each of which cost 17,500 deutsch marks, in a cabin mockup on the ground before installing them on board the 707-430 jetliners within fifteen hours. As a visual highlight, Lufthansa christened its Boeing aircraft with the names of cities, and the cabin partitions bore historical motifs of their respective sponsor cities. Thus, no two 707 cabins were alike.

From the era of the Lockheed Super Constellation and Super Star, Lufthansa transferred the opulent Senator First Class menus into the jet age. The following description is from an internal Lufthansa article at the time: "The SENATOR menu is offered in first class. This includes festively laid serving tables, elegant silver cutlery, white porcelain, champagne glasses, red SENATOR roses, and papyrus rolls held together by a silver ring with the SENATOR emblem. In addition to select wines, choices include malossol caviar, lobster, foie gras, brook trout with creamed horseradish, oysters, eel fillets, Waldorf salad, Russian salad, chilled melon, rolled fillet of ham, champagne, and spirits—all delicacies that our passengers already know from the SENATOR service on the Super Constellation."

Even if the Senator service has adapted to the spirit of the times and the evolving tastes of the traveling public

Catwalk of Lufthansa stewardesses with the uniforms worn on the Boeing 707 in Senator First Class. *From left to right: 1961–1965, 1965–1970, 1970–1978, 1970–1978. Gregor Schläger / Lufthansa*

As is still customary today, as early as the 1960s the onboard catering was loaded into the galleys by catering lift truck. *Lufthansa*

over the past fifty years, one service detail has remained unchanged since the Boeing 707 era: to this day, every passenger is welcomed aboard Lufthansa first class with a dewy red Baccara rose.

In addition to the luxury of first class, Lufthansa also offered a less expensive economy class on the 707, with 120 seats at first, providing a small foretaste of the forthcoming mass tourism that would arrive with the later wide-body jets in the 1970s. In 1961, the cheapest Lufthansa jet ticket from Frankfurt to New York and back cost almost 25 percent less than two years earlier, when only propeller aircraft were used on this route.

CHAPTER 12
LUFTHANSA: SUPER CARGO JETS

Lufthansa was one of the first airlines worldwide to begin operating the Boeing 707-330C freighter. *Lufthansa*

In 1962, Lufthansa opened its fully automated airfreight center at Frankfurt/ Main, and only three years later Lufthansa also entered the jet age in all-cargo traffic. On November 10, 1965, the airline took delivery of its first brand-new Boeing 707-330C "super cargo jet." The freighters ordered by Lufthansa were a convertible version that could be used as a "combi" (combined passenger and freight) or pure passenger aircraft. The Boeing 707-330C was considered the most modern freighter in the world when it entered service. In the beginning, a "super cargo jet" operated six times a week on the Frankfurt–New York route. It was capable of transporting up to 30 metric tons of cargo across the North Atlantic. Its cargo hold was equipped with rolling ball plates and roller conveyors for cargo pallets, which enabled the aircraft to be loaded and unloaded quickly. The turnaround time of the Boeing 707-330C in Frankfurt was a record-breaking two hours.

The Boeing 707-330C with the registration D-ABUY was lost in a crash near Rio de Janeiro, caused by an error on the part of local air traffic control. All three members of the crew lost their lives in the accident. *Lufthansa*

German Cargo Services began operating in 1977, initially with one Boeing 707-330C freighter. The 707 fleet gradually grew to four aircraft, which by 1985 were replaced by five Douglas DC-8-73s. *Lufthansa*

BOEING FLEET SYNERGIES

Two Boeing 707-330C freighters were already flying long-haul routes for Lufthansa when the first Boeing 727-30QC arrived in February 1967, bringing about a new era in the European airfreight market. Thanks to their identical fuselage diameters, pallets could be exchanged effortlessly between the 707 and 727 freighters. The Boeing 707-330C became the backbone of Lufthansa's cargo services. Between 1965 and 1970 the airline put into service six of these aircraft, which were later transferred to the Lufthansa cargo subsidiary German Cargo Services (GCS). It was not until 1984 that the Boeing 707 freighter chapter at GCS came to an end, when they were replaced by five DC-8-73s.

Equipped with quiet General Electric / Snecma CFM 56-2 engines, this version represented the ultimate evolution of the DC-8 series. The American company Cammacorp, which was founded solely for this purpose, converted former DC-8-63 "Super Sixty" aircraft from the relatively noisy JT-3D engines to the extremely quiet CFM power plants and equipped them with side cargo doors. A passenger version of one of these DC-8-73s even flew for a time on charter missions for Condor Flugdienst. The elegant Super Sixty from McDonnell Douglas finally ended the use of first-generation four-engine jets in the Lufthansa Group.

CHAPTER 13
LUFTHANSA: THE 707 WING LIFE EXTENSION PROGRAM

Dipl.-Ing. Harald Classen by the nose of a Boeing 707. *Wolfgang Borgmann*

He knew the technical peculiarities and details of the Boeing 707 like hardly anyone else: Dipl.-Ing. Harald Claasen, "Mr. 707." After completing an apprenticeship as a machinist, he began his professional career in 1958 as an aircraft mechanic with Lufthansa aircraft maintenance at Hamburg. With the arrival of the first Boeing 707 at the aircraft maintenance center, he realized that it represented an epochal quantum leap in the development of civil aviation. To learn more about the development and design of this new, modern aircraft, he decided to study at the engineering school in Hamburg. After successfully completing his studies, he was again employed by Lufthansa as a test engineer in the technical control department and was assigned, among other things, to supervise the construction of the last three Boeing 707s and the first three Boeing 747s at the Boeing plants in Renton and Everett. On the basis of his experience, he was appointed systems engineer in the field of aerostructures—especially for the Boeing 707—at Lufthansa's Technical Directorate. This fulfilled his silent wish to learn more about the problems associated with aging commercial aircraft and the measures necessary to extend their life

Checks on the number 2 engine of a Lufthansa Boeing 720B. *Author's archive*

Engine test run by Boeing 707-430 D-ABOB in the first dedicated noise control hangar at the Lufthansa base at Hamburg. *Lufthansa*

span to avoid catastrophes like that of the de Havilland DH. 106 Comet 1.

Through his intensive and responsible involvement in the program to extend the service life of the wing on the Boeing 707, the so-called Wing Life Extension Program (WLE), Harald Claasen also became highly regarded in international circles as "Mr. 707." The late Wolfgang Mayrhuber, who during his career with Lufthansa served as chairman of the executive board of Lufthansa Technik, of the Lufthansa Group, and chairman of the Lufthansa Supervisory Board, and who died in 2018, remarked appreciatively: "He earned this title." As part of his activities surrounding the maintaining of aging aircraft, the "Aging Aircraft Program," Harald Claasen contributed his expertise to the structural task groups created for this purpose and was appointed cochairman for the Boeing 707 aircraft type by Boeing. The program's focus was on the introduction of a series of measures to control and prevent corrosion damage to key areas of the aircraft structure.

THE WING LIFE EXTENSION PROGRAM

The tragic accidents involving the de Havilland DH. 106 Comet had led to a change in design regulations that also affected the design of the Boeing 707. Constructive changes had to be made in the area of the pressurized cabin and in tests carried out to verify the fail-safe nature of the structure. For the rest of the structure, Boeing had agreed with the authorities and the initial operators of the 707 to ensure that the fatigue strength was verified through operational experience and special analysis evaluations. This decision required that manufacturers, operators, and aviation authorities had to jointly carry out an intensive exchange of information about the collected findings of evaluations and repairs as part of a mandatory reporting system.

Lufthansa opened the "butterfly hangar" at Frankfurt on March 29, 1960, just before the initiation of regular Boeing 707 flights from Frankfurt. It was used to maintain the airline's new Boeing 707 jets. *Lufthansa*

Although less than ten years had passed since the first Boeing 707 had entered service, the first cracks had begun appearing in the wing structure of numerous aircraft. Particularly serious was a crack about 1 meter in length that had formed in the upper wing planking under a bea-vertail-like reinforcement and could be discovered only if there was a fuel leak. In 1965, Boeing acquired a retired 707 after about 15,000 flights to dismantle the wing into its individual parts and subject it to a thorough examination in the laboratory, using nondestructive testing methods. The findings showed that the rear spar of the wing was too weak in the area of the load application of the landing-gear forces, and that the wing spar and the wing top paneling had to be replaced with reinforced new parts. Furthermore, it was necessary to open all holes at the separation points of the individual wing parts between the inner wing, outer wing, and wing center section, as well as the tank rib in the area of the beavertail reinforcement, and to check for cracks by nondestructively using eddy currents. Then the holes had to be reamed to the next oversize bore and resealed with new oversized bolts. For the installation of the rear-spar upper belt, tapered bolts were used to achieve a work-hardening effect through pretensioning, which has an influence on service life.

As in many overhaul shops around the globe, the upper surfaces of the wings of the Lufthansa Boeing 707 fleet were reinforced in the Hamburg workshops with the help of a kit supplied by the manufacturer. The described work steps show that a high level of quality was required in the preparation and execution of the work. The Lufthansa engineers had carefully developed their own method of supporting the wings with the aid of several hydraulic jacks, in such a way that the wing structure could be held practically load free, without internal stresses and without distortion. This enabled a sealing compound to be applied to the connecting bolts during installation. The resulting

With the "Wing Life Extension Program" (WLE) in the 1960s, the Lufthansa Technical Department began doing business with external customers. The WLE thus paved the way for today's Lufthansa Technik AG as one of the world's leading aviation technology companies. *Lufthansa*

connection was absolutely fuel tight, and therefore tank leakage was eliminated. With the implementation of the WLE program, Boeing was able to extend the guaranteed service life of the Boeing 707 to the order of 60,000 flying hours and 20,000 flights. The quality and timeliness of the WLE program on the Boeing 707 are regarded as the birth of the Lufthansa technical department's external customer business and thus laid the foundation for Lufthansa Technik AG as one of the world's largest overhaul, maintenance, and repair operations in the aviation industry.

CHAPTER 14
DOUGLAS DC-8 IN LUFTHANSA SERVICE
THE EXOTICS

Although Lufthansa was a convinced Boeing customer, it could not avoid the temporary use of the Douglas DC-8, the Boeing 707's chief competitor, on its route network. The liaison with Boeing's archrival began in 1965, when, from May to December of that year, Lufthansa flew the DC-8 prototype with the construction number "1." Painted in full Lufthansa colors and bearing the American registration N8008D, the German airline leased "Ship One" from the US commercial airline Trans International Airways (TIA) for the 1965 summer season. In December 1960 the jet had been upgraded from the original prototype version of the DC-8-11, with four Pratt & Whitney JT4 engines, to DC-8-51, standard with JT3D-1 turbofans, and was fitted with a passenger cabin. In addition to Lufthansa, before it was retired in 1982 the DC-8 prototype was flown by Aeromexico, Canadian Pacific, and Delta Air Lines. It was not until 2001 that it was scrapped at the Marana aircraft graveyard in Arizona.

In 1965, Lufthansa leased the DC-8 prototype, which had been fitted with a passenger cabin, to bridge capacity bottlenecks. The aircraft was operated in full Lufthansa livery with an American registration. *Lufthansa*

The Lufthansa subsidiary German Cargo Services replaced its dated Boeing 707-330C freighters with DC-8-73s, which were almost as old but had been equipped with more modern, economical, and quiet CFM-56 power plants. The last aircraft left the fleet in 1997. *Kühne & Nagel*

In the summer months of 1985 and 1986, Condor Flugdienst leased a DC-8-73 from German Cargo Services. The aircraft was equipped with a passenger cabin for use in passenger service. *Condor*

The next use of a DC-8 by the Lufthansa Group took place in 1968, after the merger of what was then the Lufthansa subsidiary Condor Flugdienst with Südflug, founded in Stuttgart in 1953. The airline, which had been created by Rulf Bückle, had—from its modest beginnings as a provider of sightseeing flights over the capital of Baden-Württemberg—become a respected airline with a good reputation in the industry. Initially, four-engine Douglas DC-7Cs were the backbone of the airline, which operated charter flights to the Mediterranean and the Canary Islands on behalf of tour operators. Business was so good at first that Bückle planned to expand further with an all-jet fleet. To this end he ordered DC-9-32 medium-haul jets and also agreed with Swissair on the acquisition of two used Douglas DC-8-32 long-haul aircraft, which the Swiss had helped develop. However, Douglas ran into delivery problems, and Swissair did not receive its new aircraft on time. As a consequence, Swissair kept its DC8-32s for almost a whole year longer than agreed—and Südflug had to look for a costly replacement aircraft, since the planned capacity had already been sold to tour operators. The jets leased in the United States did not meet the expectations of Bückle and his customers, either in terms of cabin equipment or the service and punctuality offered on board. But he had no other choice, since not only his Südflug but many other airlines around the globe were stuck in this no-fault capacity bottleneck and no better aircraft were available to bridge the waiting time. The immense leasing costs led to huge losses that finally led Rulf Bückle to give up and sell his airline to the Lufthansa Group. It didn't help that Südflug finally took charge of the two jets with the German registrations D-ADIR and D-ADIM after all, on December 23, 1967, and March 15, 1968, respectively. After the official transfer of the company shares on January 2, 1968, the two DC-8 jets continued to fly for Südflug, which had merged with Condor, until the end of the year, when they were taken over by the German charter airline Atlantis.

However, this did not mean the end of the liaison between Condor and the DC-8. In the summer months of 1985 and 1986, the charter airline rented a McDonnell Douglas DC-8-73CF from the Lufthansa cargo subsidiary German Cargo Services (GCS) for use on passenger flights. The aircraft was flown by GCS cockpit crews, and before transporting passengers it was equipped with a comfortable, Condor-standard passenger cabin with 252 seats. Except for the large deactivated cargo door on the main deck, there was nothing to suggest the aircraft's actual purpose as a carrier of airfreight consignments on behalf of the Lufthansa Group. Registered as D-ADUC, the aircraft was originally built in 1969 as a DC-8-63CF for the American cargo airline Seaboard World and in 1983was converted by Cammacorp to the 73CF version with quieter and more-fuel-efficient CFM-56-1 engines. By January 1985, GCS had replaced its last Boeing 707-330Cs with five DC-8-73CFs, which remained part of the fleet when German Cargo Services was renamed Lufthansa Cargo Airlines on May 1, 1993. The last DC-8-73CF, with the registration D-ADUE, left the Lufthansa Cargo fleet in mid-1997, marking the end of the sporadic use of the DC-8 as an exotic aircraft in the Lufthansa Group.

CHAPTER 15
THE LUFTWAFFE'S BOEING 707S: THE GERMAN AIR FORCE ONE

The German Federal Ministry of Defense's executive transport flight took off into the jet age in November 1968, with the first of four brand-new Boeing 707-307C aircraft. The four-engine jets, which were delivered as passenger-freight versions with a side cargo door, gradually replaced the Douglas DC-6B propeller-driven aircraft previously used by the executive transport flight based at the military base at the Cologne/Bonn airport. Until the last one was retired from service in 1999, aircraft 10+01 "Otto Lilienthal," 10+02 "Hans Grade," 10+03 "August Euler," and 10+04 "Hermann Köhl" became familiar backdrops for the arrival of German government officials during state visits, but also for news reports on aid flights to crisis and disaster regions of the world.

Special events included the first visit by a member of the German government to the Middle Kingdom, when in October 1972 the then foreign minister Walter Scheel flew to Beijing aboard one of the executive transport flight's 707s. Extraordinary use was made of the four-engine jets

Fascinating photo of a 707 of the executive transport flight at its home base at the Cologne/Bonn airport. *R. Sonntag*

Produced before the aircraft was delivered to the Luftwaffe, this illustration by Boeing artists depicts aircraft 10+01 Otto Lilienthal, which was preferred for most state visits by federal German presidents and chancellors. *Boeing*

"Thumbs up" for the next mission by 10+03 August Euler. *Bundeswehr/Oed*

The executive transport flight's Boeing 707s were overhauled by Lufthansa
Technik at its Hamburg workshops. *Lufthansa Technik*

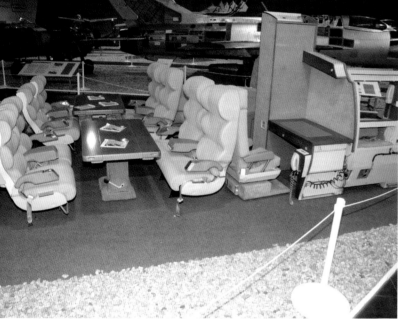

Mounted on pallets, the VIP and communications compartment for use during trips by members of the federal German government could be loaded onto any of the four Boeing 707 combi aircraft operated by the Luftwaffe. *MHM Airport Berlin-Gatow, photo: Ralf Walter Heldenmaier*

in September 1974, when Portuguese refugees had to be evacuated from Angola. During the airlift between Lisbon and Luanda, one Boeing 707 flew a total of 2,252 people out of Angola to Portugal. In the nineties, aid flights were made to various African countries and to Skopje and Tirana for refugees from Kosovo.

Aircraft 10+01 Otto Lilienthal in particular was equipped with special VIP and communications equipment, and it was the preferred choice for transporting the chancellor and members of the government on overseas state visits. One particular "frequent flier" who became famous for his global-traveling diplomacy died in 2016 at the age of eighty-nine. He was former foreign minister Hans-Dietrich Genscher, who held this post almost continuously from 1974 to 1992. Even if aircraft 10+01 was the government's preferred jet, all four of the Boeing 707s could be converted in a very short time from a VIP version to a 169-passenger version or freighter. For this purpose, the entire cabin interior was mounted on pallets, which in turn were moved on slide rails and rollers in the fuselage and could be loaded and unloaded via the side cargo door.

After taking delivery of five Airbus A310-300s from Interflug and Lufthansa, the Bundeswehr's executive transport flight parted with its tried-and-tested Boeing jets and in 1998 handed over aircraft 10+01 Otto Lilienthal and 10+04 Hermann Köhl to the NATO E-3A Airborne Early Warning and Control Systems (AWACS) squadron, stationed at Geilenkichen. In 1999, another "Zero Seven" with the serial number 10+02 went to the US Air Force, where it was converted into an E-8C Joint STARS flying command post, which is still in service today. The last remaining 707-307C, 10+03, was sold to Air Gulf Falcon of the United Arab Emirates. At the time this book was being written, it was parked and slowly rotting on the airfield of the emirate of Sharjah. Gone forever is the German Air Force One, aircraft 10+01 Otto Lilienthal, which was scrapped at Davis Monthan Air Force Base several years ago.

After it was withdrawn from service by the Bundeswehr, the former 10-04 Hermann Köhl served as a trainer cargo aircraft (TCA) with NATO at Geilenkirchen until it was finally retired in 2011. In January 2019, it was serving the Luftwaffe's Wehrtechnischen Dienststelle 61 (Technical and Airworthiness Center for Aircraft) at Manching as a training aid for prospective aviation mechanics. *Wolfgang Borgmann*

The 707 with the German tactical code 10+02 went to the US Air Force in 1999 and there was converted into an E-8C Joint STARS flying command post. It remains in service to this day. *US Air Force photo / Senior Airman Andrew Lee*

Aircraft 10+04 Hermann Köhl, which was sent to the training workshop of Wehrtechnische Dienststelle 61 (Technical and Airworthiness Center for Aircraft, or WTD 61) of the German air force at Manching, Bavaria, fared better. It has been there since 2011, serving as a training aid for prospective aircraft mechanics and electronics technicians, who are trained by WTD 61 for the military and civilian markets.

The cabin interior of the former Hermann Köhl in 2015. *Wolfgang Borgmann*

The analog cockpit of a KC-135 (*above*) compared to the current cockpit of a modernized E-3A operated by NATO. *Boeing*

Two former 707s of the executive transport flight served as training aircraft for NATO crews flying E-3A AWACS (Airborne Early Warning and Control System) aircraft from Geilenkirchen. In December 2018, Boeing completed the modernization of the last of fourteen E-3A aircraft with digital cockpits and modernized AWACS equipment. This modernization will ensure that NATO AWACS meet current and future air traffic control and navigation requirements. Five digital displays were installed in each aircraft, replacing the analog instruments from the 1970s and providing the crew with individually configurable engine, navigation, and radar data. The first aircraft thus modified were converted by Boeing in Seattle, while the remaining thirteen were configured by Airbus Military at Manching. *Boeing*

CHAPTER 16
OTHER "SEVEN O SEVENS" IN THE GERMAN-SPEAKING WORLD

In the German-speaking countries, civil Boeing 707s were flown not only by Lufthansa but also by what was then its subsidiary Condor Flugdienst and three other West German charter airlines. In Austria the elegant four-engine jet flew in the liveries of the national carrier Austrian Airlines and of Montana Austria, while Phoenix Airways operated a single Boeing 707 in Switzerland.

AIR COMMERZ
NOT A COMMERCIAL SUCCESS

Founded in August 1970, the German charter airline's head office was not far from the Hamburg airport. The small airline's base of operations was also located at the Hanseatic city's airport, and for two years it operated a small fleet of two Vickers V.808C Viscount turboprop airliners and two Boeing 707-138Bs. In a brochure from 1972, the charter airline's management lauded the flexibility of its fleet. The two V.808Cs it acquired from Aer Lingus were two of just three Viscount combis built. With a large cargo door on the main deck, they were capable of carrying either freight pallets or passengers.

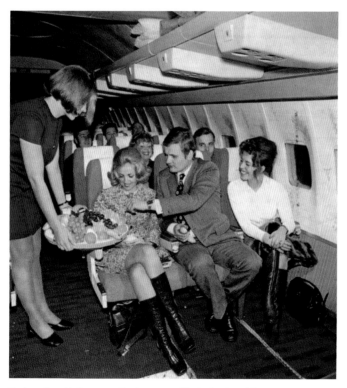

On board an Air Commerz Boeing 707-138B. *Author's archive*

With this prospectus, Air Commerz tried unsuccessfully to attract new investors and thus fresh capital for the company's continued existence.
Author's archive

In the summer of 1972, Air Commerz briefly leased one of its 707-138Bs to Merpati Nusantara Airlines. Shown here is one of the Indonesian airline's aircraft of the same type, which was also originally delivered new to Quantas.
Jon Proctor

The Boeing jets, equipped with 166 seats, had originally been delivered new to Quantas Airways of Australia in 1959, and on April 6 and May 13, 1971, they received their German registrations D-ADAQ and D-ADAP. Quantas retired the two jets in 1968, and Air Commerz acquired the aircraft from Standard Airways in the United States. When it came to its four-engine jets, the airline's management also felt that it had an advantage over its competition, since the 707-138B's four powerful Pratt & Whitney turbofan engines enabled Air Commerz to operate from smaller airports, whose runways would have been too short for the BAC 111 twin jet, then poplar among charter airlines.

With Flugkapitän Gerhard Wasserkampf as flight operations manager and John Vincent as captain in charge of training, Air Commerz employed two longtime Lufthansa pilots. As the charter airline proudly noted in one publication, Wasserkampf had been active as head of training for the airline's flight personnel since its founding, while Vincent could look back on ten years of Lufthansa line experience before joining Air Commerz as its 707 training captain. John McEvoy, the airline's chief flight engineer, was a longtime Boeing employee who brought with him fifteen years of experience as a flight engineer on the 707. It was not only the two Boeing jets that had an Australian past—deputy flight operations manager Robert Crenian had previously been employed by Quantas and TAA on the fifth continent. But all the flying skills of its key personnel could not hide the fact that the small airline, which operated mainly guest worker flights between Düsseldorf and Istanbul with its 707s, was not a commercial success.

Orders from major tour operators failed to materialize, and occasional subcharter orders on behalf of other airlines were not enough to bring about a significant improvement in the balance sheet. To bring some money into the company coffers, in the summer of 1972 Air Commerz briefly leased a 707 to Merpati Nusantara Airlines of Indonesia. After the funds ran out and maintenance work carried out by Aer Lingus could not be paid for, the latter seized one of the company's two Boeing 707s at Dublin on September 1, 1972. Three days later, all flights had to be suspended. There was no capital left for a new start, and so Air Commerz was dropped from the commercial register in January 1973.

AUSTRIAN AIRLINES
SHORT-LIVED LONG-RANGE DREAMS

As early as 1966, the management of Austrian Airlines (AUA) decided to enter the long-haul business. At the time, it was said from their board circles "that North Atlantic traffic had a surefire future and that even regional crises and armed conflicts could only have a limited impact on transport volumes." Two years later, on June 11, 1968, the AUA supervisory board authorized the managing board to conclude negotiations with the Belgian airline Sabena for the lease of a Boeing 707-329 with 146 seats.

For two years, the Boeing 707 leased from Sabena flew in the livery of Austrian Airlines and with an Austrian registration. *Austrian Airlines*

First-class service on board the Austrian 707. *Austrian Airlines*

AUA's 707 operation was ill fated from the start, as an article in the news magazine *Der Spiegel* of April 12, 1969, shows. The article states that the 707-329, painted in AUA colors, arrived in New York, the destination of the premier flight on April 1, 1969, two hours late, since it had been forced to make an unscheduled landing at Bradley Air Force Base in Connecticut. On board were forty-five guests of honor and three paying passengers, for whom Austria's federal chancellor, Josef Klaus, waited in vain at New York's John F. Kennedy Airport. As an explanation for the delay, the Austrian state secretary for information, Karl Pisa, who was traveling on the aircraft, drew up a press release with the crew that blamed headwinds, overloading of the aircraft, and the failure to obtain clearance to land as the primary reasons for the Boeing's nonarrival. This critical article made big waves in Austria, and AUA complained to the editors of *Der Spiegel* about its publication, but the article seemed to have correctly portrayed the events of the first of April.

After just two years, on April 1, 1971, AUA terminated its lease agreement with Sabena and returned the 707 to Brussels. This was due to disappointing load factors on the flights between Vienna and New York of 32.7 percent in 1969 and 34.4 percent in 1970. It was not until April 1989 that Austrian Airlines ventured to resume flights to New York with Airbus A310 long-haul aircraft, and to Tokyo shortly afterward. This was the real beginning of the intercontinental route network that AUA now operates as part of the Lufthansa Group with its Boeing 767-300ER and 777-200ER aircraft.

CALAIR
THE AIRLINE THAT NEVER REALLY GOT AIRBORNE

Frankfurt-based Calair Transportflug planned to begin operations with five 720-025s leased from Boeing in the spring of 1971. The aircraft had previously been operated by Eastern Air Lines and were initially prepared for use by Calair by the Swiss maintenance company Jet Aviation in Basel. Among other things, the five aircraft were given their distinctive blue-and-white corporate colors there. The planned takeoff date was thwarted by a delay in certification by the German Federal Ministry of Transport. Of necessity, tour operators with whom Calair had already signed contracts for the 1971 summer season began looking around for alternatives in the market, which were plentiful at the time as a result of the wave of new charter airlines then being formed. Calair, on the other hand, was left empty handed and could survive only by occasionally renting out its large Boeing jets for individual charter flights. By the end of 1971, it was already clear that the company's sporadic income was far from adequate to cover its costs. This flight adventure ended after only one year with the suspension of operations in March 1972, and insolvency two months later. Some 500 Calair creditors had invested around fifty million deutsch marks in the company, which they now had to write off for lack of assets.

Calair chose the Basel-Mulhouse airport, which was little used at the beginning of the 1970s, for training flights by its crews. In this photo taken in June 1971, Boeing 720-025 D-ACIP is taxiing out for another local flight. *Nicky Scherrer*

CONDOR FLUGDIENST
THE CRANE'S VACATION AIRLINE

On March 29, 1956, a pilgrimage to the Holy Land marked the start of the holiday airline that is now known as Condor, which is among the best-known German airlines and part of the Anglo-German Thomas Cook travel group. The ten-hour maiden flight of the Vickers Viking with thirty-six American pilgrims on board was indeed under the sign of the Condor—but under the name Deutsche Flugdienst GmbH. It was founded on December 21, 1955, by Deutsche Lufthansa, the German Federal Railways, and the shipping companies Hapag and Norddeutscher Lloyd. In 1958, the German steamship company Hansa joined as a further shareholder.

The name "Condor" was first secured by the entrepreneur Rudolf A. Oetker for his company, Condor Flugdienst GmbH, founded in Hamburg in 1957. In 1958, it began flight operations with two Convair CV 440 Metropolitan aircraft. Oetker offered Lufthansa the opportunity to buy the airline, which at the time was jokingly referred to as the "Pudding Airline" (a reference to Oetker's food company), in 1961. That is how today's Condor got its name in a roundabout way on November 1, 1961. The name refers to the Brazilian Lufthansa subsidiary Syndicato Condor Ltda., founded in 1927.

As early as 1956, the airline's flight program included Majorca and Tenerife, destinations that are still among Condor's most popular destinations. Only one year after the start of operations—and despite the already strong competition in the German charter market—Flugdienst GmbH expanded vigorously. As well as a fourth Viking, five Convair CV 240s were also added to the fleet. In early 1958, Deutsche Flugdienst chose Frankfurt Rhine/Main as

The Boeing 707-330C with the registration D-ABUJ flew for Lufthansa as a cargo aircraft, but after its conversion with a passenger cabin it also flew vacationers to overseas destinations served by Condor. *Lufthansa*

Service on board a Condor Boeing 707-430 in the 1970s. *Condor*

its home airport, to which it has remained loyal to this day. Just one year later, technical support for the fleet was taken over by Lufthansa, which also became the sole shareholder in autumn 1959.

The year 1961 not only went down in the company's history as the year it was renamed Condor Flugdienst; with two Vickers V. 814D Viscount turboprops taken over from Lufthansa, the young charter airline also entered a new era. The first Viscount, registered D-ANIP, was ceremoniously handed over by Lufthansa to Condor in Frankfurt on November 2, 1961. Immediately after the speeches, it took off on its maiden flight in the new Condor Flugdienst colors for Tenerife. In the midst of the German "economic miracle," the economy was booming. Unemployment statistics for 1964 showed a total of just 102,800 people unemployed—with 680,000 job vacancies. Germans had money and increasingly treated themselves to holidays by plane, from which Condor profited in no small measure. In 1965, the company's first jet, a Boeing 727-30, joined the fleet, which now also included two Fokker F.27 Friendship turboprops. That year, 160,000 passengers flew under the sign of the Condor—more than 100,000 of them to Mallorca alone. In 1967, Condor took over the first of three Boeing 707-330B intercontinental jets. It was D-ABOV Duisburg, originally delivered to Lufthansa. D-ABUG Essen joined the fleet in 1970, while D-ABUF Hannover was taken out of service by Lufthansa only in 1978 and then handed over to Condor. The charter subsidiary also operated the former Lufthansa 707-330C D-ABUJ Africa and the two 707-430s D-ABOC Berlin and D-ABOF München, flying them on charter routes to the United States, Asia, and South America.

MONTANA AUSTRIA
THE CHALLENGER

The Vienna-based airline, formally known as Montana Flugdienst GmbH, existed from 1976 to 1981, operating two former Qantas Boeing 707-138Bs and a 707-396C originally built for the Canadian airline Quebecair on long-haul flights, mainly to tourist destinations in Thailand and the United States. Its jets were also used on cargo flights and on behalf of other airlines. Montana Austria came to an inglorious end after the American authorities discovered that it was involved in arms smuggling for the South African apartheid regime. Not only was the crew arrested at Houston, Texas, on May 12, 1981, but the Boeing 707-396C was confiscated as well. As a result of this and other scandals, the heavily indebted airline filed for bankruptcy in July 1981.

In the foreground is the Montana Austria 707-138B with the registration OE-INA at the Vienna airport, while to its left the company's 707-396C awaits a new flight assignment. The latter aircraft was seized by American authorities in the United States after it was found to be involved in arms smuggling, which heralded the end of the airline. *Flughafen Wien AG / Thomas Gamharter*

PANINTERNATIONAL
ENDED BY DISASTER

Founded in Munich in 1968, Paninternational tried its luck in the German charter flight business with four British BAC 111-500s and two Boeing 707-123Bs. Like their twin-engine sisters, the Boeing jets with the German registration numbers D-ALAM and D-ALAL were acquired from American Airlines and mainly carried holidaymakers and guest workers between Germany and destinations in southern Europe. To finance their air fleet, the Paninternational founders exploited German tax legislation, which allowed freelancers to invest as limited partners in the loss-making airlines and reduce their own taxable income by allocating their shareholdings. It is a practice that high-earning dentists and architects used on a large scale, and so-called "depreciation" airlines such as Air Commerz, Aviaction, Calair, and Pan International sprouted like mushrooms at the end of the 1960s and beginning of the 1970s.

The dream of an expanding Paninternational ended in a tragic way with the crash of BAC 111-500 D-ALAR on September 6, 1971, shortly after taking off from Hamburg-Fuhlsbüttel. Among other things, the airline's chaotic technical organization had led to the tank for the water-injection engine's thrust-augmentation system for cooling the two Rolls-Royce Spey engines during takeoff being filled with highly flammable jet fuel instead of demineralized water. As a result, the engines of the charter aircraft, carrying a full load of passengers, caught fire immediately after takeoff and failed completely shortly afterward. Captain Reinhold Hüls managed to put the aircraft down on the nearby A7 motorway, but it then struck an overpass and broke apart. Of the 121 people on board, twenty-one passengers and one crew member died. Paninternational ceased operations shortly after the disaster, and the two Boeing 707-123Bs returned to American Airlines in the United States.

PHOENIX AIRWAYS
THE ONLY SWISS 707

Like the German airline Paninternational, Phoenix Airways, founded in 1970 by private investors in Switzerland, operated the BAC 111 and Boeing 707. In contrast to its German counterpart, however, the charter airline based at the Basel-Mulhouse airport had just one example of each type: a BAC 111-500 with the registration HB-ITL and the Boeing 707-131F HB-IEG. For the duration of the conversion to the "F" combination version with a side cargo door by Israeli Aircraft Industries in Tel Aviv, Phoenix rented a further 707-131 from the Israeli aviation group between March and October 1972, with the American registration N732TW. Both aircraft were originally delivered by Boeing to the US airline TWA before being used to fly tourists from Switzerland to destinations around the Mediterranean, as well as on long-haul routes to Asia and Africa, on behalf of travel companies. The aircraft was converted into a combi-freighter so that it could be used to transport fruits and vegetables from Israel to western Europe during the winter months. In addition to tourist charter flights, Phoenix Airways also leased its two jets to other airlines and travel agencies for ad hoc operations. High costs, not least due to the oil crisis at the time, forced Phoenix to cease operations in March 1974.

As of the autumn of 2018, Boeing 707-131F HB-IEG was the only "zero seven" ever registered in Switzerland.

Aircraft D-ALAL, shown on a company postcard, was one of the German charter airline's two 707-123B airliners. *Uwe Timm collection*

Phoenix Airways was the only airline to operate a Swiss-registered Boeing 707. This photo shows the airline's HB-IEG taking off from Basel-Mulhouse in August 1973, on a charter flight to Palma de Mallorca. *Christoph Hartmann*

CHAPTER 17
THE END OF THE 707-400

In Germany, unitl the summer os 2021, the last preserved Boeing 707-400s with Rolls-Royce engines were located at the international airports of Hamburg and Berlin. A 707-307C, equipped with Pratt & Whitney engines, is permanently gounded and used for technical training at the Bavarian air base at Manching. However, the only exhibit of the 707 era that is still open to the public is the nose of a former American Airlines aircraft, which is on display in the Deutsches Museum in Munich. The jets once preserved in Berlin, Hamburg, and the museum cockpit in Munich are featured below, while the Boeing used at Manching for technical training is described in detail in the chapter on the 707s operated by the Luftwaffe.

707-458 GERMAN MUSEUM OF TECHNOLOGY, BERLIN-TEGEL AIRPORT

The Boeing 707 parked for many years at the edge of the Berlin-Tegel airport has sadly been scrapped in May 2021, just days after the final decommissioning of Tegel airport. What began in 1986 as a flying gift from Boeing to Lufthansa on the occasion of the delivery of the 200th Boeing jet to the German airline has developed over the years into an incomparable tragedy. Initially parked as a shining exhibit in front of the passenger terminal in Tegel, the jet soon had to move twice on the airport grounds and found it last resting place in an area of the airport that was visible neither to passengers nor visitors. Neither Lufthansa, which found no use for the gift and immediately passed it on to the Berlin-based aircraft collection of the Deutsches Technikmuseum, nor the museum, which would have preferred to have rejected the gift due to the high maintenance costs associated with it, nor the Berlin-Tegel airport, on whose property the Boeing rested, had any interest in the slowly rotting veteran. Although painted in historical Lufthansa colors with the correct registration D-ABOC and name "Berlin" from 1960, this 707-458 was not a historic Lufthansa "Jet Intercontinental" but a former aircraft of the Israeli airline El Al with the construction number 18071 and the original registration 4X-ATB. After its retirement, Boeing acquired the four-engine airliner and painted it in historical Lufthansa colors. With Lufthansa lettering and crane symbols covered with tape for this one flight, Boeing pilots flew the jet, wearing an American registration, from Frankfurt through one of the three Allied air corridors to

The Boeing 707 that was pushed off to the edge of the Berlin-Tegel airport was a forlorn sight. It was originally a gift from Boeing to Lufthansa, but the German airline had no interest in it. *AirlinerSpotter*

In this photo from the 1970s, D-ABOD appears in Lufthansa's then-current livery. *Lufthansa*

In 1999, on the occasion of its eightieth anniversary, the Hamburg airport acquired the former Lufthansa Boeing 707-430 D-ABOD for the symbolic price of one German deutsch mark. The jet had already been taken out of service in 1976 and served for two decades as a training aid for prospective aircraft mechanics at Lufthansa Technik in Hamburg. *Michael Penner / Flughafen Hamburg GmbH*

Berlin, where the 707 landed at Tegel on November 22, 1986. This trick was necessary because until German reunification in 1990, the only aircraft allowed to land in West Berlin were those of the victorious powers of World War II—France, Great Britain, and the United States. The jet, "unmasked" after its arrival, was received in Tegel by the then-current mayor of Berlin, Eberhard Diepgen; Lufthansa CEO Heinz Ruhnau; and Boeing president Thomas A. Wilson. Although this was not an original Lufthansa aircraft, it was the first landing in Berlin by an airliner painted in Lufthansa colors since the Second World War.

BOEING 707-430 FLUGHAFEN, HAMBURG GMBH

This Boeing 707-430, originally delivered to Lufthansa as D-ABOD and wearing, in its final days, the registration of its sister aircraft D-ABOB, was clearly visible to visitors to the Hamburg airport's viewing terrace. After its retirement

from passenger service, it was removed from the civil aircraft registry on March 19, 1976, but served for two more decades as a training aid for aspiring aircraft mechanics of Lufthansa Technik in Hamburg. Around 1,700 trainees learned their craft, among other things, through D-ABOD. Most of the time, the Boeing was a proverbial "flying classroom," but in the 1980s the curious Lufthansa staff started two of its four engines for a test run on the ground, in which 70 percent of maximum engine power was achieved. After that, the Rolls-Royce Conway turbofan engines fell silent forever. Because of the financial costs and effort required to maintain the old-timer in good condition, which with time became ever greater, and the adoption of new training methods that made the 707 unnecessary, Lufthansa Technik decided to sell the aircraft to the Hamburg airport on its eightieth birthday in 1999 for the symbolic price of one deutsch mark. As a final task, Lufthansa Technik trainees painted the 707 in the airport's red and white colors, which the jet was to keep for many years. As soon as it was taken over, the airport's 707, which was given the fictitious registration D-AFHG, became

These photos of the Flughafen Hamburg GmbH's 707-430 museum aircraft were taken on August 12, 2000. *Wolfgang Borgmann*

a popular background motif for photo shoots, promotional and television productions, and motion pictures. Its film career began as early as 1976, when Bavaria Filmstudios asked Lufthansa if it was possible to rent the aircraft for a production at what was then the Munich-Riem airport. Lufthansa agreed, and so D-ABOD was converted for a short time into the US presidential aircraft "Air Force One" on just one side of the fuselage, after approval by the American authorities. Lufthansa demanded 60,000 deutsch marks from the film studio for this performance. This included the restoration of the aircraft (which was mothballed in Hamburg) to airworthiness for a hoped-for sale, the flights from Hamburg to Munich and back again, landing fees, and then represervation at Hamburg. The 707, which wore a fictitious Lufthansa livery and D-ABOB registry when it was scrapped in 2021, was used for simulated accident exercises at the Hamburg airport and is kept able to move for this purpose—albeit only in tow, and not under its own power. Parts of the demolished aircraft were sold by auction and its nose section is planned to be transformed into a fully operational flight simulator. In this way at least a small part of this worldwide last preserved Boeing 707-400 will continue to live on with fans of this vintage Lufthansa "Boeing Jet Intercontinental."

707-123 NOSE SECTION AT DEUTSCHES MUSEUM, MUNICH

In the exhibition of the Deutsches Museum on Museum Island in Munich, the nose section of a former American Airlines Boeing 707-123 can be seen, with a view into the cockpit of the jetliner. In homage to the use of this type of aircraft by Lufthansa, the nose was painted in the historical Lufthansa colors of 1960. In the autumn of 2021, this was the only 707—or at least part of one—that was accessible to the public in Germany.

CHAPTER 18
BOEING 720 IN USE BY THE FAA AND NASA
CRASH FOR IMPROVED FLIGHT SAFETY

A commercial aircraft bursting into flames on landing is a frightening image. But in this case, it was a test carried out by the US space agency NASA in cooperation with the US Federal Aviation Administration (FAA). Their goal: to improve aviation safety. The dramatic images of the burning Boeing were taken on December 1, 1984, at NASA's Dryden Air Force Test Center at Edwards Air Force Base, California. Under remote control, with no people on board, the FAA-retired Boeing 720 was deliberately flown into obstacles on the ground, which caused the full fuel tanks to burst. The aim of this "controlled-impact demonstration" was to test an additive added to the Jet-A aviation fuel, which showed promising fire-retardant properties in smaller test setups. Rapidly spreading fires after emergency landings, it was hoped, could be nipped in the bud, increasing the chances of survival for passengers and crew after a crash.

The test engineers erected various steel masts at Rogers Dry Lake at Edwards Air Force Base to tear open the fuel tanks housed in the wings during the collision. The Jet-A fuel contained therein was mixed with the fire-retardant FM-9 additive, which had to be filtered out again before

combustion in the four Pratt & Whitney JT3C-7 engines due to the threat of clumping—and thus engine failures. In addition to the fuel tests, NASA investigated the behavior of new fire-retardant and shock-absorbing materials on seats, cabin windows, side panels, and galleys, and to protect flight data recorders. Instead of real passengers, crash test dummies sat in the passenger cabin. They were equipped with countless measuring devices to measure the physical loads in an air accident. The Boeing 720's final flight was preceded by four years of planning for the deliberate crash, which the involved FAA experts deemed potentially survivable. The Dryden Flight Experimental Center developed the remote-control system for the aircraft, the engine manufacturer General Electric took care of protecting the engines against the expected clumping of the additive, and the FAA determined the optimal mixture of Jet-A fuel and the FM-9 additive. In the fall of 1984, NASA tested all systems in fourteen flights with test pilots on board. In the event of a failure of the already active remote-control system, they could have intervened and brought the machine to the ground safely under manual

This series of photos shows the sequence of the failed test of a flame-retardant additive to increase the chances of surviving an aircraft accident. *NASA*

control. These flights were controlled by NASA test pilot Fitzhugh Fulton, who flew the Boeing from a flight simulator at Dryden. Well prepared by these test flights, Fulton was at the virtual controls on December 1, 1984, and the Boeing 720, which had previously been fueled with 74,957 pounds of jet fuel, took off with no one on board. After takeoff, Fulton initiated a left turn and let the aircraft climb to a maximum altitude of 2,296 ft. In order to simulate an emergency landing as realistically as possible, the flight plan called for a landing with the undercarriage retracted. The aircraft was to fly down the extended runway centerline toward the test facility in order to leave the fuselage undamaged for as long as possible. Everything seemed to go as planned at first, but then the left wing suddenly dropped and touched the ground. Fulton was unable to compensate, and the Boeing began to slide toward the steel beams at an angle of 45 degrees. One of the engines struck first and immediately burst into flames. As a result of the impact, the machine continued to spin and hit the next obstacles almost sideways, causing the damaged right wing to break off, and it was hurled across the fuselage by the force of the impact. Within a few seconds, the Boeing was enveloped in a fireball, which took an hour to fully extinguish. If it had been a real air accident, the occupants' chances of survival would have been zero, contrary to the hopes of FAA experts. After the officials had overcome their disappointment at the disastrous end of the test flight, NASA and FAA immediately halted the development of the additive and its planned use in aviation. Even more far-reaching, however, was the realization that laboratory tests are no substitute for practical tests. The shocking end of the Boeing 720 was nevertheless a win for aviation safety, the improvement of which has not been studied exclusively in laboratories since then.

CHAPTER 19
BOEING 707 AND 720
SPECIFICATIONS

Type	Wingspan	Length	Height	Power Plants	Max. Takeoff Weight	Max. Fuel Capacity	Max. Seating Capacity	Cockpit Crew
Boeing 707-120	39.88 m. (130.8 ft.)	44.22 m. (145 ft.)	12.70 m. (41.7 ft.)	4× Pratt & Whitney JT3C (JT3D)*	B version 117,000 kgs. (257,940 lbs.)	65,590 liters (17,327 gal.)	174	4 (including navigator on long-range flights)
Boeing 707-420	43.40 (142.4 ft.)	46.61 m. (152.9 ft.)	12.72 m. (41.7 ft.)	4× Rolls-Royce Conway	141,700 kgs. (312,395 lbs.)	90,160 liters (23,818 gal.)	189	4 (including navigator on long-range flights)
Boeing 707-320B	43.40 m. (142.4 ft.)	46.61 m. (152.9 ft.)	12.85 m. (42.2 ft.)	4× Pratt & Whitney JT4A	141,700 kgs. (312,395 lbs.)	90,160 liters (23,818 gal.)	189	3
Boeing 707-320B	44.42 m. (145.7 ft.)	46.61 m. (152.9 ft.)	12.83 m. (42 ft.)	4× Pratt & Whitney JT3D**	148,500 kgs. (327,387 lbs.)	90,290 liters (23,852 gal.)	189	3
Boeing 707-320C	44.42 m. (145.7 ft.)	46.61 m. (152.9 ft.)	12.80 m. (42 ft.)	4× Pratt & Whitney JT3D	151,500 kgs. (334,000 lbs.)	90,290 liters (23,852 gal.)	194 (combi version)	3
Boeing 720	39.88 m. (130.8 ft.)	41.30 m. (135.5 ft.)	12.62 m. (41.4 ft.)	4× Pratt & Whitney JT3C	104,000 kgs. (229,280 lbs.)	60,900 liters (16,088 gal.)	149***	3
Boeing 720B	39.88 m. (130.8 ft.)	41.68 m. (136.75 ft.)	12.55 m. (41.2 ft.)	4× Pratt & Whitney JT3D	106,200 kgs. (234,131 lbs.)	61,300 liters (16,193 gal.)	149****	3

* For 707-120B version
** For intercontinental version
*** Optional seating for 156 with installation of two additional Type III emergency exits above the wings
**** Optional seating for 156 with installation of two additional Type III emergency exits above the wings
Source: Boeing

CHAPTER 20
THE COMPETITORS

The Convair 880 was created at the initiative of Howard Hughes, who was looking for a tailor-made jet for his Trans World Airlines (TWA). However, it proved to be too small to compete with the Boeing 707 and Douglas DC-8.
Jon Proctor

The following examples of the numerous turboprops and jetliners of the 1950s, 1960s, and 1970s competing with the Boeing 707 are the Convair CV 880, Douglas DC-8, and Vickers VC10. None of the three patterns even managed to come close to the success of the Boeing intercontinental jet.

CONVAIR CV 880 GOLDEN ARROW

Consolidated Vultee Aircraft Corporation, or Convair for short, was a name well known to the traveling public, especially in Europe. In the 1950s and 1960s, their very comfortably equipped Metropolitan airliners were operated by Iberia, Finnair, Lufthansa, SAS, and Swissair, among others, and were regarded as synonymous with relaxed flight in the "golden age" of air transport. Unlike the two major American aircraft makers, Boeing and Douglas, in the mid-1950s Convair had close contacts with one of the most dazzling figures in American aviation: Howard Hughes. As the first billionaire in US history, oil tycoon, film producer, and aviation entrepreneur, he asked Convair management if it could develop and

Type	Maker	First Flight	Number Built	Wingspan	Length	Height	Power Plants	Cruise	Range	Crew
CV 880	General Dynamics / Convair, San Diego, California, USA	27 Jan 1959	65	39.58 m (129.8 ft.)	39.42 m (129 ft.)	11 m (37.4 ft.)	4 × General Dynamics CJ-805-3	ca. 990 kph (615 mph)	ca. 4,400 km (2,734 mi.)	3
Douglas DC-8-32*	Douglas Aircraft Company, Long Beach, California, USA	30 May 1958	57 (556 all versions)	43.46 m (142.6 ft.)	45.90 m (150.6 ft.)	12.90 m (42.3 ft.)	4 × Pratt & Whitney JT4A-9	ca. 885 kph (550 mph)	ca. 6,450 km (4,007 mi.)	
Vickers VC-10**	Vickers-Armstrong Aircraft Ltd.	29 Jun 1962	54	44.55 m (146 ft.)	48.36 m (158.7 ft.)	12.04 m (39.5 ft.)	4 × Rolls-Royce Conway 540	ca. 900 kph (559 mph)	ca. 8,000 km (4,971 mi.)	3–4

* Specification = Swissair DC-8-32 version

** Specification = Standard VC-10 version

manufacture a transcontinental-range jet for Trans World Airlines (TWA), which he controlled. If Convair management had known at that time that Howard Hughes's allure would lead not just to orders, but also to the threat of ruin for the Convair aircraft plants, the CV 880 might not have been produced in the first place.

But in the hope of winning a large piece of the civilian jet market, in 1956, after numerous design studies, Convair unveiled the final design of the jetliner, called "Skylark 600." The Tool Company (Toolco), part of the Hughes empire, through which Hughes acquired all TWA aircraft and leased them to the airline, signed preliminary contracts with Convair and General Electric on June 7, 1956, for more than thirty examples of the jetliner, now christened the Golden Arrow. On the same day, Delta Air Lines followed with an order for ten aircraft; however, Toolco, as a larger customer, was free to determine their delivery time.

Convair got its first taste of Howard Hughes's eccentric ideas when he demanded that the plane be built out of golden shimmering metal.

However, the jet, now called the Golden Arrow, remained an obsession, since there was no manufacturing process at the time that could guarantee an even, golden coloring of all the fuselage and wing panels. When the first two customers, Toolco (TWA) and Delta Air Lines, converted their purchase intentions into fixed orders for a total of forty aircraft on September 10, 1956, there was no longer any mention of the Golden Arrow. Instead, the aircraft project had by then been given its final name, Convair 880. With a cruising speed of almost 621 mph, the 880 is still to this day one of the fastest passenger aircraft.

After this initial meddling in the aircraft program, Convair was about to learn what it meant to do business with Howard Hughes, especially during the production phase. Production of the first aircraft had progressed well at the Convair plant in San Diego, and nothing stood in the way of the contractually agreed-upon delivery of the jets to TWA and Delta between the fall of 1959 and September 1960, when in July 1959 a team of Toolco inspectors appeared unannounced on the final-assembly line. The first two CV 880s, destined for TWA, which were due for delivery in November and December 1959, aroused their particular interest. This was done without the knowledge of the TWA management, who learned about the events only via their own team on-site! The situation worsened dramatically in a surreal way when in October, the team of inspectors arrived accompanied by armed security guards, who sealed off both machines. No Convair or TWA employees were allowed to approach the aircraft, let alone enter them. Continuing the final assembly process was out of the question. As it turned out, a few days after the Toolco guards laid siege to the Convair production building, Howard Hughes had personally issued the order for this action. Convair managed with difficulty to keep the final-assembly line running and was able to deliver at least the first CV 880 to Delta Air Lines on February 9, 1960. However, the drama surrounding the aircraft destined for Toolco dragged on throughout 1960. Hughes categorically refused, without giving a reason, to accept the 880 fleet destined for TWA.

It seems like an act of desperation that TWA bought one of the planes ordered by Toolco with its own money in May 1960, in order to at least use this CV 880 as a crew trainer for the hoped-for commissioning of the remaining twenty-nine aircraft. The situation for TWA eased only on December 30, 1960, after Howard Hughes lost control of the airline as a result of financial problems. On the same day, Toolco transferred the delivery positions for nineteen CV 880s to TWA, the first of which was handed over to the airline just two days later. By January 18, 1961, the fleet had grown to five, including the training machine, which the airline had already taken over in May 1960. Freed from the handicaps imposed by Howard Hughes, Convair set about the speedy completion of the remaining jets, previously "trapped" on the final-assembly line.

TWA began regular service with its new Convair airliners on January 12, 1961. Within days, the new flagship of the TWA fleet began setting one speed record after another; for example, on January 24, 1961, on the route from Chicago to New York. With an average speed of 680 mph, the flight time was just one hour and eleven minutes. The Convairs, christened "StarStream880" by TWA, were initially equipped with eighty-five first-class and just twenty-nine coach-class seats. In the forward cabin area, a lounge with twelve armchairs also invited first-class passengers to have a drink above the clouds. In addition to its extremely luxurious seating, the CV 880 also impressed with its sophisticated cabin design. Harley Earl, chief designer of General Motors and "father of the GM Corvette," was commissioned by Convair to design a passenger cabin to counteract the oppressive tube effect from the perspective of passengers in the rear rows of seats. His recipe: he lowered the cabin roof by a few centimeters, creating an optical subdivision into smaller segments.

Despite all its progressive ideas, Convair's CV 880 was not a success. Howard Hughes was not innocent in this, his reckless conduct having plunged the CV880 final-assembly line into chaos while refusing to allow Convair to use its completed machines for demonstration flights to potential customers. In order to make it possible to successfully market its jet, Convair produced just sixty-five examples of the CV 880 basic model and the further-developed CV 880M at a loss. Nevertheless, the CV 880 deserves a place among the legendary jetliners because its design was so attractive that renowned airlines around the world placed orders for it. These included Cathay Pacific, Civil Air Transport, and Japan Air Lines in Asia, and the Venezuelan airline VIASA in Latin America. In the United States, in addition to Delta and TWA, Alaska Airlines and Northeast also purchased brand-new aircraft. The CV 880 also flew in KLM and Swissair liveries in Europe. The latter used the Convair jets as a transitional solution pending delivery of the larger CV 990. On the other hand, "Lisa Marie"—the CV 880 owned privately by Elvis Presley—became world famous. It can now be seen in the Museum of the King of Rock 'n' Roll in Memphis, Tennessee.

DOUGLAS DC-8

Company patriarch Donald Wills Douglas Sr. was in no hurry for his aircraft company, founded in 1920, to enter the jet age. Unlike Boeing, the Douglas Aircraft Company had a remarkable order cushion of 275 DC-6 and DC-7 propeller airliners when, on the far side of the Atlantic, the British de Havilland Comet 1, the first production passenger jet in the world, entered service in 1952. Donald Douglas was also unsure whether, after a global investment of around 1.5 billion US dollars in new propeller aircraft, the airlines would be willing to replace these aircraft with faster jets within a few years. After all, this would cause their fleets to lose massively in value, and the airlines would suffer considerable losses.

C. R. Smith, president of American Airlines, one of Douglas's major customers, was skeptical about the new jet propulsion. Instead, he urged Douglas to develop the Curtiss Wright 3350 piston-engine DC-7 propeller airliner to knock out the even-slower Lockheed L-1049 Super Constellation, operated by its rival Trans World Airlines. The DC-7 project was launched in 1951, while preparations for the jet era were in full swing in the UK and Canada, and Boeing was already working on plans for a first civilian jet commercial aircraft.

Scandinavian Airlines System (SAS) was one of Douglas's most loyal customers, operating DC-4s, DC-6s, DC-6Bs, DC-7Cs, and DC-8-32s and -55s on its long-haul network over the years. Douglas developed the extremely long-range DC-8-62 version especially for the SAS polar route between Copenhagen and Los Angeles. DC-8-63s and DC-10-30s rounded off the order for Douglas and McDonnell Douglas long-range jets by SAS. SAS

Although he had invested large sums in the new, old-technology DC-7, Donald Douglas wanted to keep at least one foot in the door to the approaching era of jet air travel. In June 1952, he established a small project office in Santa Monica, California, to prepare studies for a possible jetliner for the company. For Douglas, what was at stake was nothing less than the existence of the company, which had already fallen behind Boeing at this early planning stage.

Whomever the Douglas engineers spoke to, opinions as to the correct size of the project now called DC-8 differed widely. Pan American in particular pushed for a jet whose dimensions would be comparable to those of the Boeing 367-80 Dash 80 experimental aircraft, officially announced in April 1952. Other airlines, on the other hand, preferred a smaller jet with less seating capacity.

Boeing and Douglas's plans were made possible by development of the Pratt & Whitney JT3 commercial engine, which was derived from the J57 military power plant. Both Boeing and Douglas had already gained a wealth of experience with the J57 in their own military jets and therefore counted on the reliability of the civilian JT3 for the first versions of their four-engine passenger aircraft.

While the de Havilland Comet was withdrawn from service in April 1954 as a result of material fatigue and a spectacular series of crashes, Boeing launched its 367-80 Dash 80, which later resulted in the civilian Boeing 707 and the military KC-135, just three months after the British jetliner was grounded. On the other hand, Douglas, which had fallen behind due to the initial hesitation on the part of the company patriarch, had at that time little more to offer than initial designs and a wooden model, albeit full size, of the aircraft's fuselage.

THE SETBACK

Douglas could not afford an experimental aircraft like the Boeing Dash-80 of its archrival from Seattle for cost reasons. All the more reason for the managers in Santa Monica to hope for a tender from the US military for a tanker in the DC-8 category. If one of its designs was chosen, this would absorb some of the enormous development costs and thus ensure the continued existence of the entire company. The shock was therefore all the greater when, in February 1955, Boeing was commissioned by the US Department of Defense to supply 21 KC-135 tankers. While Boeing was able to use this order to cross-finance not only the KC-135 but also its Dash-80 experimental aircraft and development of the civil 707, Douglas had to bear all the costs associated with the DC-8 himself. However, if the company wanted to continue to play an active role in civil aircraft design, there was no alternative but to continue the DC-8 project.

Douglas initially offered interested parties a DC-8A domestic version for continental routes within the United States, with deliveries to begin in 1956 at the earliest, and a DC-8B overwater variant for international routes between the continents starting in 1958. On October 13, 1955, Pan American president Juan T. Trippe announced the order for twenty-five of the overwater version of the DC-8 with advanced Pratt & Whitney JT4 engines. At the same time, he ordered just twenty Boeing 707-120s, which at that time were still offered with the narrower passenger cabin of the Dash-80 and KC-135. It was therefore limited to just five seats per row, instead of six as in the DC-8. The future seemed particularly bright for Douglas after Trippe announced that he planned to order more DC-8s in place of Boeing 707s in the future.

Just twelve days after Pan Am, United Air Lines placed an order for thirty DC-8s, followed by Dutch KLM as the first overseas customer. By the end of 1955, Douglas's order books had filled with other orders from such prominent customers as Eastern Air Lines (26), National Airlines (6), Japan Air Lines (4), and Scandinavian Airlines (7). Pan Am was not the only airline for whom the larger cabin width was a decisive factor in favor of the DC-8. United Air Lines also favored the Douglas jet. However, the cards were reshuffled between Boeing and Douglas when American

Based at Frankfurt am Main, the German charter airline Atlantis flew two used DC-8-33s and three brand-new DC-8-63CFs (*photo*) from Germany to destinations in North America between 1969 and 1972. *Author's archive*

Airlines was able to convince Boeing management to widen the fuselage of its four-engine jet to six seats per row at the latest. The best argument for this was an order for thirty Boeing 707s from American on November 8, 1955.

Development of the DC-8 dragged on longer than Douglas had originally planned. In June 1956, the company announced that it was building a new final-assembly line in Long Beach, California, specifically for the DC-8. The first aircraft parts were built in September 1956, and next

to the production hall Douglas built a huge water tank for material fatigue testing, capable of accommodating a complete DC-8 fuselage. After the fatal crashes of the de Havilland Comet resulting from metal fatigue, Douglas had provided the DC-8 with small crack stoppers made of titanium on the fuselage panels as well as all recesses, such as doors, service flaps, and windows. After 113,000 simulated flights in the water tank, the first cracks appeared on an aluminum window frame, but these were halted by the stoppers as planned, with a large safety margin. By the time of the DC-8's first flight, the engineers had simulated 120,000 flights with the pressurized cabin activated and ended the program after another 20,000 uneventful takeoffs and landings. The DC-8 had successfully demonstrated its reliability.

AIRCRAFT FAMILY

The prototype of the new Douglas design, dubbed Ship One, first took to the skies on May 30, 1958. After an extensive test flight program and certification by the US FAA on August 31, 1959, the type's first customers, United Air Lines and Delta Air Lines, began using their already delivered DC-8-11s on scheduled services on September 18, 1959. This domestic version was followed by the DC-8-20, -30, -40, and -50 series, a variety of other variants with identical fuselage lengths but different engines and ranges. The first major evolutionary step was the DC-8 Super Sixty models DC-8-61, -62, and -63, with extended fuselages. The -62 and -63 series also had Pratt & Whitney JT3D fan engines housed in sleek engine pods. In addition, there were aerodynamically revised wings and a much-longer range—in the case of the DC-8-62, this was about 6,213 miles.

The Scandinavian airline SAS not only was the driving force behind the DC-8-62 development, the details of which were determined in a Stockholm hotel room by SAS and Douglas representatives, but also placed the first order for four series -62 machines on April 4, 1965. As pioneers of polar air traffic, SAS was looking for a jetliner that could travel the distance between Scandinavia and the US West Coast nonstop, a task for which Douglas had tailor-made his DC-8-62.

In addition to SAS, many other European airlines, such as Alitalia, Finnair, Iberia, KLM, Swissair, and UTA, were among the largest customers for this four-engine jet, which was extremely popular with passengers and crew. In Germany and Switzerland, the DC-8 was used by charter airlines such as Atlantis, Balair, and Südflug for many years, and in August 1965, even Lufthansa rented the DC-8 prototype for charter flights to North America.

After it became apparent in the 1970s that stricter noise regulations would be coming into force, especially in the United States, various North American airlines asked Douglas to offer quieter engine options for their DC-8s, which had been in service for many years. Pratt & Whitney offered its then-new JT8D-209 engine, while Cammacorp, founded by retired Douglas managers, offered the much-quieter and more economical CFM-56-1 to upgrade the DC-8 versions -61, -62, and -63. After United Air Lines and Flying Tiger Lines opted for the Cammacorp concept, further orders from Delta Air Lines and Cargolux, among others, quickly followed. In 1981, the US FAA approved the models now known as DC-8-71, -72, and -73. Among the early operators of the DC-8-73 was Lufthansa cargo subsidiary German Cargo, which brought its five aircraft into Lufthansa Cargo AG, which was founded in 1994. One of them was temporarily equipped with a passenger cabin in 1985–86 and rented to Condor for its charter flights to North America.

TECHNICAL REFINEMENTS

The DC-8 features some technical features that distinguish it from most of its generation's jets. Cabin pressure is not generated directly by engine bleed air, as on the Boeing 707, but by a complicated process in the nose of the jet. In the beginning it is the same as modern jet engines: bleed air is taken from a compressor stage of the DC-8's engines, but it drives a turbine, which in turn is coupled to a compressor. This draws in outside air and compresses it until the required cabin pressure is achieved. The background was the fear shared by Boeing and Douglas designers that the Pratt & Whitney JT3 engines had leaky bearings from the very beginning, and that oil fumes might contaminate the cabin air. This is an issue that has lost none of its explosiveness to this day! The air intakes for these four compressors installed in the nose of the aircraft gave the DC-8 its characteristic "smile."

Up to the DC-8-50, the initial versions also had a hydraulically castoring main undercarriage, which reduced turning radius when the plane was maneuvering on small airport aprons. Another special feature of the DC-8 was also connected with its undercarriage. Located above the starboard main undercarriage, engine number 3 could be started when no ground power unit was available. A pressure line was installed in the undercarriage, through which compressed air from the shock absorbers was fed into the engine, which thus enabled it to start. The onboard battery supplied the electricity for the ignition of the combustion chambers. If engine number 3 started, it was then used to start the remaining three. It was a procedure rarely used in practice, with just one attempt being made.

Douglas attached great importance to the design of the DC-8's cabin. Jack Graves, who was assigned this task, had already designed the interior of all Douglas airliners, beginning with the DC-4. He achieved an advanced, modern concept in the DC-8 but also preserved a touch of the old propeller era in the jet age. It would therefore have been theoretically possible to fold beds down from the cabin ceiling on night flights, as in the "golden age" of air travel. Similar to the propeller-driven airliners of the 1950s, the first DC-8 versions also had curtains, instead of blinds, on the cabin windows.

Douglas had the Palomar passenger seat designed especially for the DC-8. It included all the usual supply facilities, such as fresh-air nozzle, call button for cabin crew, folding table, and oxygen mask for emergencies. A fluorescent reading lamp was also attached to the side of each headrest. The individual seats were attached to the cabin floor and to the side of the cabin wall. This lateral mounting accommodated the supply lines for electricity and air. As a result, the seats could be flexibly moved in the cabin or replaced quickly. Another curiosity: the armrests of passengers seated by the windows were not on the individual seats, instead being mounted on the side panel. They were

in one piece, from the first row to the last, running lengthwise through the cabin. Douglas patented the Palomar seat, which was installed in every DC-8 passenger jet up to the 50 series.

Compared to the Boeing 707, the DC-8 has relatively few—but larger—cabin windows. They are optimized for the 40-inch spacing of the backrests. Douglas had taken the first-class seating of American airlines as a model for this in the 1950s. Despite the maker's good intentions, however, in later years, with much-tighter seat distances—especially in the economy class—this led to some "window seats" having no window, causing frustration among passengers.

The DC-8 reached the market too late, but Douglas made it a big success. The excellence of its design is confirmed by the fact that at the time of the publication of this book, of the 556 machines of all versions built between 1958 and 1972, some examples are still in daily use as freighters and even as a NASA research aircraft.

VICKERS VC-10

The Vickers VC10 is a great example of British engineering in the 1950s and 1960s. At the same time, however, it is also representative of a misguided industrial policy that led to expensive aircraft projects being developed in postwar Britain, which missed the global market.

The VC10 was the second long-distance design that Vickers-Armstrongs attempted to develop in the 1950s. The last remnants of the VC7 long-haul jet, canceled in 1955, had just been cleared from the Vickers-Armstrongs aircraft factory production halls for scrapping when the British state airline, BOAC, invited manufacturers de Havilland and Vickers to discuss a new attempt at a British long-range airliner.

The failure of the VC7 in the first place was due, among other things, to the complete misjudgment of the future of air transport by BOAC chairman Sir Miles Thomas. He predicted in 1955 that the first American jet would not fly over the North Atlantic before 1962. He thus saw no hurry to enter the jet age, instead opting for the British-made Bristol Britannia turboprop airliner for long-haul services. In fact, it would not be seven but only three years that would pass before Pan American flew away from BOAC's outdated de Havilland Comet 4 with its modern Boeing 707 jets.

The four-engine Vickers VC7, derived from the Valiant V bomber, was originally designed for the Royal Air Force as the V-1000 troop transport. It was to be capable of carrying up to 120 people in its 144 ft. fuselage over a distance of almost 2,485 miles. In January 1953, the British Ministry of Procurement ordered a prototype, followed in June 1954

by an order for six production machines. It was envisaged that the aircraft would be powered by the then-new Rolls-Royce Conway 5 turbofan engine. Two engines would be accommodated in each wing root, similar to the de Havilland Comet. Work on the prototype began at the Vickers plant in Foxwarren and continued until the largely completed components were transferred to Wisley in preparation for the first flight, scheduled for 1956.

The first problems became apparent in the summer of 1955, when it became known that the V-1000 would be heavier than planned and that all promised performance data would no longer be met. The Ministry of Procurement

In 2018, none of the fifty-four Vickers VC10s built were still airworthy, but enthusiasts were able to book seats on board a Super VC10 once used by BOAC, British Airways, and the Royal Air Force at the Cold War Jet Days in Bruntingthorpe, UK. During simulated short-takeoff runs at maximum thrust, they experienced how four Rolls-Royce Conway aircraft sounded and felt in the VC10 cabin. *Wolfgang Borgmann*

subsequently lost interest in the project, which was halted by government decree on November 29, 1955. This was followed by months of futile attempts by interested airlines and British politicians to persuade the government to reconsider its decision—all components, including the almost completed fuselage, as well as all of the production facilities, were therefore scrapped from 1956.

In the meantime, the competitive situation in North Atlantic air transport had changed completely. The Boeing 707 became available much sooner than Sir Thomas had predicted, and BOAC, now without the prospect of a modern British long-haul jet, ordered fifteen examples of this American design on October 24, 1956. Since the 707 was intended exclusively for North Atlantic traffic, BOAC was also looking for a suitable aircraft type for its British Empire routes to Africa and Asia. This was the starting point when BOAC placed a large order for thirty-five standard VC10s from Vickers on January 14, 1958, with options for twenty additional machines. The new VC10 design was not a dusted-off VC7, but a completely new concept that slowly took shape on the drawing boards of the Vickers-Armstrongs designers at the Weybridge plant. BOAC required that the VC10 be capable of safely taking off with a full payload even from runways that were too short for the still-underpowered Boeing 707 and Douglas DC-8. The result was a tailor-made aircraft design with uniquely good short-takeoff characteristics, which, however, came at the cost of a higher empty weight. This was caused by the large wings of the VC10, which were equipped with an ingenious high-lift system consisting of leading-edge slats that spanned the entire wing, and large trailing-edge flaps. Combined with its four powerful Rolls-Royce Conway engines, which were actually overpowered for this design, the VC10 met all the expectations set in it and was ideally suited for the BOAC network. For example, a standard VC10 was capable of flying nonstop from Nairobi to London with fifty-nine paying passengers and their luggage, while a BOAC Boeing 707-430 could not have done so even without a single passenger on board!

Everything seemed to be developing positively for the VC10 project when BOAC signed a contract with the British Aircraft Corporation (BAC), of which Vickers became a part in 1960, on June 23 of that year, for ten examples of the extended Super VC10. This was initially designed as a 212-passenger long-haul jet in economy class, whose fuselage was stretched by almost 29.5 ft. compared to the basic version. BOAC planned to use this Super VC10 on North Atlantic routes starting in 1965. Shortly after signing the contract, however, BOAC insisted on a shorter fuselage, lengthened by just 13 ft., so that it could also use its "supers" economically on other routes with lower traffic volumes.

Vickers management had no idea at this point that the conversion of the original BOAC order from thirty-five standard VC10s into fifteen "Standard" and thirty Super VC10s would set in motion a dynamic that would have almost ended the program, and thus a déjà vu for Vickers to the failed VC7. On January 1, 1964, Sir Giles Guthrie became the new chairman of BOAC. One of his first tasks was to get the company, which was losing money, back on track—and so he planned to reduce the fleet and cancel the thirty Super VC10s, which he considered superfluous! However, since BOAC was state owned, Guthrie did not have the final say on this point. And so, after mediation by the British government, the airline reduced its order by "just" thirteen machines, to seventeen Super VC10s. Three more aircraft were issued to the British Royal Air Force as transport aircraft—but the remaining ten Super VC10s of the original BOAC order were canceled.

BOAC received its first standard VC10, with the registration G-ARVI, on April 22, 1964. The following day the aircraft received its certificate of airworthiness from the UK Civil Aviation Authority, and the second aircraft, with the registration G-ARVJ, was handed over to BOAC. From day one, the elegant airliners did exactly what BOAC had once ordered them for.

The two VC10 variants were particularly popular with passengers. Due to its large wings, whose aerodynamics were not disturbed by engine gondolas as on other types, the VC10 flew extremely quietly. This also applied to cabin noise, which, thanks to rear engines, radiated only marginally into the cabin. For example, BOAC advertised with the slogan "A Little VC10derness" to highlight the outstanding passenger comfort on board the elegant four-engine jet.

In addition to the British airlines BOAC and British United Airways (BUA), the standard and Super VC10s were also flown by various airlines in the Middle East and on the African continent. Some standard VC10s were also used as VIP jets in the Persian Gulf region. After the last civilian VC10s retired from line service in the early 1980s, they continued to fly with the Royal Air Force until a few years ago as troop transports and aerial-refueling tankers. It was not until September 24, 2013, that the final landing of a Vickers VC10 took place at Bruntingthorpe airfield near Birmingham. The fact that this type, with only fifty-four aircraft completed, was not a sales success is due to its being too closely tailored to the original requirements of BOAC. Thus, the VC10 was tailor-made for the route network of the airline that would have preferred never to have put it into service.

This historical BOAC postcard shows the silhouette of one of its Super VC10s. *Author's archive*

THE AUTHOR
WOLFGANG BORGMANN

Wolfgang Borgmann's enthusiasm for aviation was passed on to him by his parents, who were active in the aviation field. In his early years, he began building up an aviation historical collection that provides numerous rare photos and documents, as well as exciting background information, for his books. Since April 2000, Borgmann has been active as an author and freelance aviation journalist. He lives in Oerlinghausen, Germany. His website is: www.aerojournalist.de.

Boeing 737
A Legends of Flight IllustratedHistory
ISBN: 978-0-7643-6138-8 $29.99

Airbus A300/310
A Legends of Flight IllustratedHistory
ISBN: 978-0-7643-6139-5 $29.99

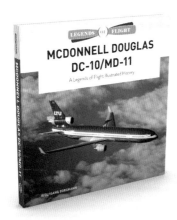

McDonnell DouglasDC-10/MD-11
A Legends of Flight IllustratedHistory
ISBN: 978-0-7643-6137-1 $$29.99

Boeing 757
A Legends of Flight IllustratedHistory
ISBN: 978-0-7643-6346-7 $29.99